THE FILMMAKER'S GUIDE TO CREATIVELY EMBRACING LIMITATIONS

Starting out as a filmmaker comes with a host of limitations and restrictions leading to one key question: how do you channel your creativity past these daunting challenges to create compelling and impactful films? Authors William Pace and Ingrid Stobbe advise the key is to not consider them roadblocks to being creative, but opportunities. Providing both historical and contemporary examples, as well as outlining practical exercises filmmakers can apply to their own creative processes, they illustrate how filmmakers can transform obstacles into successes.

Looking into limitations and restrictions arising at all stages of the film production process, the book illuminates the importance of developing unique creative muscles and how to apply them to your own work. This is a unique text in the field that provides both a theoretical and practical approach to inspired and savvy filmmaking that uses limitations as points of inspiration. Drawing on examples from artists like Frank Oz, Pete Docter, Gabby Sumney, and Shaun Clarke, filmmakers will gain a well-rounded understanding of the creative processes behind motion picture production and learn how to shape their own independent creative voice when utilizing budget-conscious, creatively aware filmmaking. Foregrounding limitation-embracing strategy and capability, making a film for the first time or with limited resources is no longer overwhelming with this highly practical textbook.

Ideal for undergraduate students of film production and first-time filmmakers.

William Pace is an alumnus of NYU's acclaimed graduate Film & TV program and has written five distributed independent feature films (four of which he co-produced), various TV episodes, and several optioned screenplays. He also directed the award-winning feature film "Charming Billy," plus several award-winning short films, including "A Relaxing Day" (written by Pulitzer-nominated playwright Theresa Rebeck). He continues to work professionally as well as serve as a Faculty

Associate of Digital Media Production at Seton Hall University in New Jersey, USA, where he teaches screenwriting, film & TV production, and editing.

Ingrid Stobbe is an Associate Professor of Digital Filmmaking at Lesley University's College of Art & Design in Cambridge. She is an Advisor to the board of Women in Film & Video New England, as well as an former editorial board member of the Journal of Film & Video, and previously served on the Marketing Committee for the Metropolitan New York Chapter of the US National Committee for UN Women. She has comprehensive experience designing curricula for the visual arts, and her pedagogy has been internationally recognized – most recently including the 2021 Best-In-Track award at OLC Innovate, and the 2020 University Film and Video Association Award of Teaching Excellence. She additionally advises tenure track and full-time academic applications and regularly speaks at various institutions about media production's evolving landscape and its broader social impact.

THE FILMMAKER'S GUIDE TO CREATIVELY EMBRACING LIMITATIONS

Not Getting What You Want Leading to Creating What You Need

William Pace and Ingrid Stobbe

LONDON AND NEW YORK

Designed cover image: Kaitlyn Gernatt

First published 2023
by Routledge
4 Park Square, Milton Park, Abingdon, Oxon OX14 4RN

and by Routledge
605 Third Avenue, New York, NY 10158

Routledge is an imprint of the Taylor & Francis Group, an informa business

© 2024 William Pace and Ingrid Stobbe

The right of William Pace and Ingrid Stobbe to be identified as authors of this work has been asserted in accordance with sections 77 and 78 of the Copyright, Designs and Patents Act 1988.

All rights reserved. No part of this book may be reprinted or reproduced or utilised in any form or by any electronic, mechanical, or other means, now known or hereafter invented, including photocopying and recording, or in any information storage or retrieval system, without permission in writing from the publishers.

Trademark notice: Product or corporate names may be trademarks or registered trademarks, and are used only for identification and explanation without intent to infringe.

British Library Cataloguing-in-Publication Data
A catalogue record for this book is available from the British Library

Library of Congress Cataloguing-in-Publication Data
Names: Pace, William (Faculty associate of digital media production), author. | Stobbe, Ingrid, author.
Title: The filmmaker's guide to creatively embracing limitations : not getting what you want leading to creating what you need / Williams Pace and Ingrid Stobbe.
Description: Abingdon, Oxon ; New York, NY : Routledge, 2023. | Includes bibliographical references.
Identifiers: LCCN 2023005102 (print) | LCCN 2023005103 (ebook) | ISBN 9781032261263 (hardback) | ISBN 9781032261256 (paperback) | ISBN 9781003286639 (ebook)
Subjects: LCSH: Motion pictures--Production and direction--Handbooks, manuals, etc.
Classification: LCC PN1995.9.P7 P24 2023 (print) | LCC PN1995.9.P7 (ebook) | DDC 791.4302/32--dc23/eng/20230424
LC record available at https://lccn.loc.gov/2023005102
LC ebook record available at https://lccn.loc.gov/2023005103

ISBN: 978-1-032-26126-3 (hbk)
ISBN: 978-1-032-26125-6 (pbk)
ISBN: 978-1-003-28663-9 (ebk)

DOI: 10.4324/9781003286639

Typeset in Bembo
by MPS Limited, Dehradun

Access the Support Material: https://www.routledge.com/9781032261263

CONTENTS

Foreword   *viii*
Preface   *x*
Acknowledgements   *xi*

PT. I
Limitation Throughout History   **1**

1 The Problem of Choice: Psychology and the Effective Storyteller   3

2 Historical Limitations Throughout Film Production's Evolution Leading to Innovation   10

    2.1 World Wars, Isolation, and Storytelling 10
    2.2 Pre-Sound to Post-Sound 16
    2.3 The Hays Code and Cinema Censorship 19
    2.4 Black and White Meets Color 30

3 Film, Digital, Accessibility, and Contemporary Trends   37

    3.1 Early Photography 37
    3.2 Early Film 40

    3.3   *Early Video*   47
    3.4   *Contemporary Trends: Streaming*   56

4 From Sow's Ear to Silk Purse: Creative Victories Through Limitation   **61**

    4.1   *"Just One Word – Plastics": Pete Docter on* Toy Story   62
    4.2   *No Budget? No Problem: Maya Deren and Amateurism in the Quest for Artistic Authenticity*   66
    4.3   *"They Have No Legs": Frank Oz on the* Muppets *and Beyond*   72
    4.4   *The Martini Shot*   77

PT. II
Practical Implementation   79

5 The Why of Why: Why Is Each Element of Production Important, and How Does Limitation Aid the Visual Storyteller?   **81**

6 Exercises in Limitation: Storytelling on the Page   **84**

    6.1   *Starter Yeast*   84
    6.2   *No Dialogue – The Active Screenplay*   87
    6.3   *Less* Is *More*   91

7 Exercises in Limitation: Storytelling on Screen   **94**

    7.1   *One-Take Jolly Dolly*   94
    7.2   *A Lens by Any Other Name*   96
    7.3   *Oh What's in a Frame – Where Are the Edges?*   99

8 Exercises in Limitation: Storytelling in the Editing Room   **106**

    8.1   *5 Edits to Tell A Story*   106
    8.2   *Physical Editing: The Frame as Reversed Exquisite Corpse*   109
    8.3   *More Than Meets The Eye*   112

PT. III
Conclusions   **117**

9 The Day You Have No Limitations is the Day You Have
   No Choices   119

PT. IV
Interviews   **123**

10 Interviews With Working Artists On the Role of Limitations
    In Creating Their Work   125

   10.1   Interview Introduction   125
   10.2   Interview Excerpts with Seth Barrish   126
   10.3   Interview Excerpts with Shaun Clarke   129
   10.4   Interview Excerpts with Oliver Curtis   135
   10.5   Interview Excerpts with Pete Docter   140
   10.6   Interview Excerpts with Gretchen Hall   144
   10.7   Interview Excerpts with Frank Oz   149
   10.8   Interview Excerpts with Gabby Sumney   157

PT. V
Addendum   **163**

11 Spare Scenes for Your Use and Practice   165

Index   *173*

FOREWORD

"The most important thing about limitations for me first, for a director, is that if you don't have it, there's no juice. If you want to be a journeyman director, anybody can do that – learn the film language, learn the shots, learn the lens, you know, anybody can do that. If that's the kind of director you want to be and stay on budget exactly, and stay on schedule exactly and just shoot what you're supposed to, what the script says, OK, but there's no juice in there. You know, and the restrictions saying, No, you don't have that much time. No, the sun's going down. No, the actor's sick today. No, the crane is missing a part. No, it goes on and on and on... that's when the juice occurs. That's it. 'Holy shit, what are we going to do?' And that's where the fun happens. That's filmmaking to me. The other stuff is good craft, but the filmmaking is the juice and the excitement, saying, "Holy fuck!! Hey, how about this!?' That's the joy."

-Frank Oz

Learn the film language.

Learn the shots.

Learn the lens.

These are all vital elements of the filmmaking process, and without them we of course have no films. But we aren't here for that today, so if that is the book you are looking to find, you'll need to tuck this one into your basket and keep looking for one more to take home.

Because the unspoken gel – that "Holy Fuck" glue that holds those three pieces above to the final product – the film itself – that is what we're interested in today. That magical intermediary moment of uncertainty where filmmakers have gotten themselves to a point of experience in life – *vis-a-vis* set happenings, real life whoa I didn't think THAT could happen and it did, or just general observations of character – and all of these unspoken toolsets have become just as valuable to the new filmmaker as any of those on that list above in not simply resolving but recognizing the potential an issue has in becoming a catalyst for progress in moviemaking.

Let's say that once more – we're looking at you today to talk to you all about becoming an artist who recognizes inevitable challenges not as something to get over, but as something to befriend, understand, and expand upon as artistic launchpads for improvement.

So if it's technical skills you are looking to hone, by all means – there is a literal mountain of books, youtube tutorials, and various other directions you can find yourself able to investigate. But if it's the *je ne sais quoi* you're looking for, that little bit of edge when it comes to knowing how to handle what you will not (believe us – you won't) know that is going to come your way, and also recognizing how wonderful those moments are – please read on! Because if you're ready for a secret … the Holy Fuck is about as Holy as it gets in filmmaking, and we've got lots of great tips, industry tales, and exercises in store for you to become a great filmmaker who is ready to embrace incoming challenges as opportunities, and be open to exploring the benefits of initially limiting situations in your productions.

So put that other book in your basket if you must, but let's go!

PREFACE

This book is designed in such a way that a filmmaker should be able to move freely about it depending on the needs and interests at that moment. The foreword explains the manner in which a reader can use the book in multiple ways to make the most out of their experience, and what it contains.

Additionally, throughout the chapters, various illustrations and photos are used to augment the reader's understanding of the concept and examples discussed.

Reference material such as spare scenes, media, and other relevant course materials for the exercises will also be provided.

Additionally, edited interviews the authors conducted with noted filmmakers and film artists, such as Pete Docter, Frank Oz, Shaun Clarke, Gabby Sumney, Seth Barrish, and others on the subject of how limitations and restrictions play an essential part of their creative process are included in their own chapter.

ACKNOWLEDGEMENTS

William Pace Acknowledgments

I was that kid. The one that always had a book in his hand. All my life books entertained me, informed me, transported me, consoled me. So much so that one of the most oft-repeated phrases I recall my Dad saying to me was, "What? You got your nose in another dang book?" (I cleaned that up for you; you're welcome.) Don't go all judgey on my father; he only had 2 months of high school before he dropped out to work fulltime for the rest of his life to provide for his family. And Dad became one of the biggest supporters in my pursuit of a career in film and teaching. I only wish he was still here so he could see my nose buried deep in this one. Thanks Dad!

FIGURE 0.1 Baby Bill's 1st Book.

And anyway, it was true – I did always have my nose in a book – in fact, even before I could read. Look:

But while my Dad eschewed books, Mom was – is – a devourer of them. My hometown's local library's dedicated staff knows exactly what Mom loves to read and sets those aside for her as soon as they come in so she always gets the newest and latest. (Huge shout-out to librarians around the world for the truly special work they do!) She supported my literary love when Dad couldn't fully grasp the allure of the written word and encouraged me to read on. Thanks Mom!

The only thing I loved more than reading was movies, which I was deeply crazy about. Some of my favorite early memories are of Dad letting me stay up late to watch a movie with him on our old boxy black & white TV set, sharing a bottle of Pepsi-Cola into which we poured salted peanuts into. (Again, don't judge until you've tried it.). And there's an infamous little family story about how I had the choice between taking our beloved, beautiful collie, Lady, to a local dog show or go see the matinee of a film at our town's lone movie theater. Of course, I chose the movie. So Mom enlisted my cousin Rhonda to take Lady to the dog show. And what happened? I got a disappointing cinema experience from a less-than-stellar movie. And my cousin? She got a trophy. And $25. And her picture in the paper. And several assorted prizes when Lady won 1st Place at the dog show! Admittedly, Lady was indeed an amazing and gorgeous dog, but I certainly didn't foresee her winning a top prize that would rain down untold treasures. My mother made my cousin give me one of the lesser prizes (Crayons), as Lady was technically my dog, and ever since then my family has never let me live that down, even all these decades later. But it was a great indication of my future and how I would one day chose movies as the life I wanted to pursue.

I'll spare you all the details of that pursuit and skip right to where we are now: acknowledging and thanking those who share responsibility (blame?) for the creation of this book.

First and foremost thank you to my students: all the students I have had the privilege to teach in my extended time as a professor. I always loved school. (Yeah, I was also that kid too. I was actually upset when my next-door neighbor, Cindy Jackson, who was one year older, got to go to 1st grade while I had to wait a whole 365 more days before I could. But I made up for it by staying in school as long as possible, pursing a "terminal" degree, my MFA.) So, being able to combine my love of both movies and school as a teacher of screenwriting and filmmaking has been one of the most satisfying and gratifying aspects of my professional career. And like many teachers, I don't believe I really knew what I myself was doing until I had to teach others what to do; it forced me to look at my own processes and beliefs and figure them out in order to share them with others. And in doing so, students have consistently been my best teachers of how to teach. Thanks students!

And I wouldn't have gotten the opportunity to become a teacher if it wasn't for my New York University Graduate Film classmate, Mira Kopell – she was teaching screenwriting at The New School in Manhattan but was leaving to move back to San Francisco (with her husband, fellow NYU classmate Paul Holzman) and I literally begged her to make an introduction of me to the New School's administration so I'd have a shot at being her replacement ... and she did, and I did and they did – select me as her replacement, that is. Thanks Mira and The New School! (By the way, Mira has written her own book on screenwriting that I highly recommend.)

Another NYU classmate who has been a paramount fixture and guiding light in both my film career and my teaching profession is Tom Rondinella. Tom and I have been working together longer than most modern marriages, from painting the houses of suburban NJ for money to get through (and past) graduate school, to co-writing screenplays, to being on numerous film sets where we have swapped back-and-forth roles as director and producer (and even filmed in a brain surgery suite where someone's skull was open!) to now having teaching offices down the hall from one another at Seton Hall University ... we've been through a lot, both professionally and personally, and what I have learned from Tom is immense, enhanced by the guidance, support, and confidence he has bestowed on me. Truly, without him, I would have nothing here to write about. Thanks Tom!

And Seton Hall University (which I would not be teaching at without Tom) has been an amazing place, allowing me to teach all aspects of media making, from screenwriting to producing to film/video production to TV studio production to editing ... all of the things I love. I have felt both encouraged and supported there and I have grown so much as a teacher because of it. Thanks Seton Hall – go Pirates!

I very much want to thank all of our interviewees who were so kind to give us their time and knowledge and did so with grace, humor, and enthusiasm. Each one was a delight, and the thing they all professed was a shared belief that filmmaking truly is a collaborative process, and the best work only comes when you empower and encourage others. While not all of them may professionally teach, all are teachers in their own way and certainly taught us a lot in the writing of this book. Thank you Frank, Gabby, Gretchen, Oliver, Pete, Seth, and Shaun!

Conducting my interviews created a lot of raw material, so I want to thank Joey Nardone, one of my Seton Hall University students, who took on the chore of transcribing the interviews, which was no small chore – when all tallied up, they totaled over 100 single-spaced pages. And he didn't do it as part of a class for a grade or extra credit or anything like that; he did it because it that's the kind of great student – person – he is. Thanks Joey!

Also, in conjunction with my interviews, I want to thank Victoria Labalme, who is the nexus through which we were able to connect with many of the people interviewed. Among many amazing things, Victoria is an incredible human magnet who gets so much pleasure and fulfillment out of bringing strangers together to connect and create; truly, she has elevated it to an art form, and seeing the joy on her face when doing so is delightful. Thanks Victoria! (She also has her own inspiring book about pushing yourself beyond what you expect you can do I highly recommend: *Risk Forward: Embrace the Unknown and Unlock Your Hidden Genius*.)

If you are holding this book in any form – physical, digital, metaphorical ... you have two people to thank – and neither of them is me! The whole concept of using restrictions as a point of inspiration for filmmaking creativity began with a workshop I proposed for the University Film & Video Association 2019 annual teaching conference (UFVA is a not-for-profit organization in the United States dedicated to the promotion and study of moving image practice in higher education). I asked Ingrid Stobbe to co-teach it with me, but unfortunately, she couldn't make it, so I went and did it by myself. Awkwardly. Ask anyone who attended. It was an idea not yet fully formed. So, with Ingrid not able to participate, I sort of winged it. And when it was over, I thought, "Well ... that was interesting." And not necessarily in a good way. And that may have been that. Except...

For Sheni Kruger. At the time Ms. Kruger was an Editor, Filmmaking and Photography for Focal Press/Routledge and she too was at the 2019 UFVA conference, appearing on a book panel. I had met her once or twice while teaching at The New School, so went to the panel to see her speak. Interestingly, the name of the panel? *Publish Not Perish*, which was on how to get published. The funny thing? I had no aspiration on publishing a book. None. Zilch. As a university professor, I have definite non-curricular obligations I need to do to prove myself worthy of continuing being a professor, but as a teacher of media production, publishing a book is not one of them. I went to the panel because I knew Ms. Kruger – and, because so many of my colleagues are expected to publish – I thought it would be interesting to discover what the deal was. So I went. And it was very interesting. Enlightening. And scary! So much work to write a book and get it published! Who would want to do that? Certainly not me. But I stuck around when it was over to say hello to Ms. Kruger, and, after all the faculty who were desperate to get their manuscript published finally finished mobbing her, I went up to talk to her. And you know what she said? "Sorry I missed your workshop this morning, as it sounded very interesting. In fact ... I think it should be a book." At first I thought she was kidding me, seeing all that had just been said in the panel about the arduous process. But she wasn't. She was dead serious. She set up an appointment to discuss it more, and we did. And the thing is, the more she talked, the more I liked the idea of it. I mean, go back to the first paragraphs of this acknowledgement and look at that photo again – the idea of that kid having a book with his name on it? A little fire started in a corner of my brain. And for better or worse – you can be the judge of that when you finish this book – the fire spread. So, thank you very much, Sheni Kruger!

While I'm here talking about our publisher, I also have to thank the oh-so-patient and helpful editors who have endured shepherding this book. I, personally, am responsible for blowing at least three deadlines on delivering the manuscript, which is one of the reasons several editors have had their hand in its creation. And yet none of them ever sent a hitman out for me, which makes me admire their tenacious tolerance all the more, not to mention their wise guidance. So, thanks Rachel Feehan, Genni Eccles, Andrew Peart, Claire Margerison, and Sarah Pickles!

But the person most responsible for this book in front of you? Ingrid Stobbe. There's a reason I asked her to co-teach the initial UFVA panel with me: because she's great! Even though I'm more narrative-based and she is more experimentally based (which I think is a plus, to have two people who come at filmmaking from different angles), we share a similar sense of the mission of teaching filmmaking as a way to empower people to tell their stories and get them out in the world. And, for better or worse, we also share a similar sense of humor, as you'll soon discover in the following pages. So, once Ms. Kruger convinced me the workshop concept should indeed be a book, I immediately called Ingrid and told her, "Guess what? You didn't get a chance to be a part of the workshop, but now a publisher wants it to be a book and there's no way I'm going down that road by myself. Help!" Smartest move I made. Because absolutely, hands-down, swear on stack of whatever you want to push in front of me, this book would not exist without her. If Ingrid hadn't said yes, you'd have a bunch of air in your hands right now. Like the utterly adorable Newfoundlands her family has, she is strong, smart, loyal, gentle but unrelenting when a life – or book – needs to be saved. Even when I practically begged her to kick me to curb, she did not give up; instead, she showed what an incredibly dedicated and supportive teacher she is, talked me off the ledge, and gently guided me back to the keyboard in order for me to make my contributions. And every step of the way she was – as she always has been since I've known her – talented, funny, insightful … not to mention a promiser of custom-made cupcakes. I have co-written screenplays, and let me tell you: writing with a partner who is not on the same wavelength as you is one of the most excruciating experiences I have endured. But with Ingrid? It was like buttah, a meld(t)ing of minds focused on the same outcome: to create a book to help media-makers be as creative as they can possibly be, despite the limitations so often seem in the way. I am very eternally grateful. Thanks so much Ingrid! (But I'm still waiting for my cupcake.)

Finally … no, that's not right. Better is ultimately I must thank my wife, Hillary Bradley because without her this book – or any script I might write, movie I might make, or class I might teach – would mean nothing. Creating is about sharing; while admiring your own work can have a certain satisfaction, it is fleeting and hollow. Something created is only truly complete when you can share it with someone else – and that's even more true for life than art. I write and make movies, Hillary draws and paints; we create our visions of the world and share them with each other, serving as the first eyes of the world to experience them. But the greatest thing either of us has created is our life together – my world is fuller and more complete because of it. Without it, nothing I could create on my own would matter. That's why she is my ultimate. Thank you Hun-nee.

Ingrid Stobbe Acknowledgements

The process of creating this book has spanned years, and multiple Universities for me. As such, it has taken a broad network of support as you can certainly understand. And so whenever you have the time to read through this portion of the text, please do, because those included here were paramount to the completion of this particular project, though they may not know it.

I have to start with my parents, as I suppose so many of us do, but particularly for allowing me to pursue many different artistic venues. Had I known that filmmaking would mean writing 100+ pages single spaced I'm not sure I would've directly been interested, I'm going to spell that out right now. But already considering Writing as a path of intrigue provided a level of foundational support thanks to early efforts from Mom and Dad. I want to especially thank Mom for all the doodles on the napkins at lunch, for allowing me to paint whatever I wanted onto my bedroom walls, and for telling me to "get a grip" when things got too dramatic. I want to thank my Dad for his film knowledge, his amazing musical rolodex, and perhaps most importantly his general life approach to ridiculousness. All of which were so very needed in the highs and lows of writing a project of this scale over the span of several years. I wish very much that he could see this, but I feel confident he'd enjoy the puns.

I want to thank the late John Mannear, who was the first person to tell me I could write. He was my 11th and 12th grade English teacher, took no shit, loved films, and taught poetry by pulling stanzas from the music of our mutual love, Bruce Springsteen. His lessons could be incredibly multidimensional. I wish he was here, but if you can see this, Mr. Mannear, please know how important your words remain to my confidence as a writer, and how important it was for me to have the arts connected so fluidly that early on.

A tremendous note of thanks to the now-closed organization Pittsburgh Filmmakers, whose unique design allowed those just learning about filmmaking to join classes of a caliber accredited by Universities, in a structure that was diverse, exciting, and innovative. It was the rarest of spaces, where I learned to use a motion-picture camera, edit, and affirm that my storytelling ideas in film were valid for the first time, while working and paying out of pocket. The manner in which this organization seamlessly took down financial barriers to artistic learning and bridged elements of community in the filmmaking process was of extraordinary influence in the bones and user-flexibility of this text. In particular, Dean Mougianis, whose support meant so much to me, was integral to my progress in media.

Those at Emerson College – initially professors and now colleagues, in particular Jan Roberts-Breslin and Kathryn Ramey. Two women whom I look to always for professionalism of practice, of person, and for how to keep swimming in deep and sometimes choppy waters. I am not sure they know how much of an influence they each have been in my life, job choices, and willingness to fight for integrity in life + artistic decision-making.

My friends at Lesley University who continuously provided support and encouragement in all the forms imaginable – cupcakes, beer, hugs, words of affirmation, sometimes physically pulling me off of the floor, and constructive feedback. Kate Castelli, Jen Barrows, Emme Rovins, and Diana Direiter, you saw some moments and having you in my life has meant a great deal in general, but especially trying to wrap a long project in a tough time while working full time.

Kaitlyn Gernatt, who designed our beautiful cover, and who has been with me through the pandemic while at Lesley University, and let me get to know her and her talents as an Artist. I'm so happy we were able to work with you on this, and endlessly grateful for your support in so many other ways – I've lost count of how many cupcakes I owe you at this point, I hope you are keeping track. Your discussions and collaborations were some of the highlights for me, and your visual decisions are part of the book's essential body. I appreciate you so very much.

To all of our wonderful interviewees for believing in the project and its mission, and for lending your experiences to our readers to allow them the belief and knowledge to learn through your films, sets, observations, kerfuffles, and brilliant moments. I want to say to Gabby Sumney, Gretchen Hall, and Shaun Clarke, I'm so very happy to see you included in this book, and to have your experiences and works on the page. You've all been friends and beautiful collaborators, and to be able to have your words on a platform that allows others glimpses of the opportunities I've had working with you is such a treat.

Nicole Hart, Kat Lombard-Cook, Elizabeth Mezzacappa, JoAnn Cox, Amy Cocchiarella, Julie Eisen, Jen Casne, Danielle Zuckerman, Gretchen Mayhaus, Britta Lee, Tucker Stobbe, Katherine Shozawa, Matthew Nash, Andrew Proctor. At any given point I let out cries for help to you and to your immense credit you consistently answered, even when I was (really) caffeinated. Literally, God bless you.

Thank you Routledge, Taylor & Francis Group for supporting us in our long timeline, as we went through multiple "Oh wait a moment here's …" and ebbed and flowed through a pretty challenging few years globally along with the rest of the world. Your patience, kindness and support was consistent, and so incredibly appreciated from start to finish. Thank you for also laughing at our jokes. I know we do. Sheni Kruger, Claire Margerison, Sarah Pickles, Genni Eccles, Rachel Feehan, Andrew Peart – gosh, thank you so much for all that you did and your endless (truly) patience.

My lovely students – I love you all so much. You make me happy to come to class, and to be excited to try new things. I'm so thrilled our class work is in the book, and that your faces are there to greet the readers, so they have a sense of how I get to enjoy my day. You're the best, truly - so proud of you all and the work we do together.

And gosh, I feel like I'm forgetting someone … who could it be? Oh I know, I know! William Pace – holy cow – here we are! Thank you for asking me to hop onto a presentation way back in a South Orange, New Jersey coffee shop that became this journey into what I believe is an important work for the film community. The meetings that spanned the pandemic, the witnessing of each other's struggles through that epic arc, the ideations therefore of this work, and being in one another's lives more than perhaps we even thought possible is quite something.

Thanks for bringing me onto the Seton Hall campus in the first place and changing my life trajectory, and providing validation to my career at that stage. Thanks for all the support in my life in so many ways that you have provided since we met, I'm so glad to be your friend and colleague. I'm proud of this work, and of the landing point that it has gotten to, with you as the often hilarious co-pilot of this endeavor, and the life stages it encompassed. Truly, Thank You!

PT. I
Limitation Throughout History

1
THE PROBLEM OF CHOICE
Psychology and the Effective Storyteller

Pt 1: Clarity After Chaos
True Story:

A director was in the middle of directing their first feature film. While "only" a scrappy, gritty independent production, it was a huge deal – finally they were seeing their lifelong directing dream come true; excitement and hopes – and fears and self-pressure – were off the charts. The shoot was on a very tight budget and schedule with no margin for error, but thankfully things were going well as they headed into the final day – the production was on time, on budget and the footage looked promising; all they had left to do was shoot the critical climatic sequence. Critical, because a film's ending is what most impacts an audience's experience of a movie – it needs to be as strong as possible.

Luckily, that final morning's shooting went well. Then they broke for lunch and …

Well, first, let's back up a bit and give some context.

In movie making, there is something called "geography." No, it's not the boring stuff you may recall from earlier school years about what country lies between what bodies of water and such details. In filmmaking, geography refers to the physical layout of a scene – where everyone is physically located within a scene and its settings. For example, say we have a scene that takes place in a fancy dining room; we want to establish there is a main doorway, a large dining table in the middle of the room, and a buffet set up on a sideboard on an opposite wall next to a door that leads into the kitchen. We'll have guests coming in the main door and servers in through the kitchen door, people getting food at the buffet and at some point, the host will probably go check in on how the kitchen is doing with the meal preparation … it's a lively scene, a lot going on. But if the director (and cinematographer) does not take the time to establish all these physical logistics, it could just look like a mass of people walking randomly around here and there while those seated at the table

DOI: 10.4324/9781003286639-2

4 Limitation Throughout History

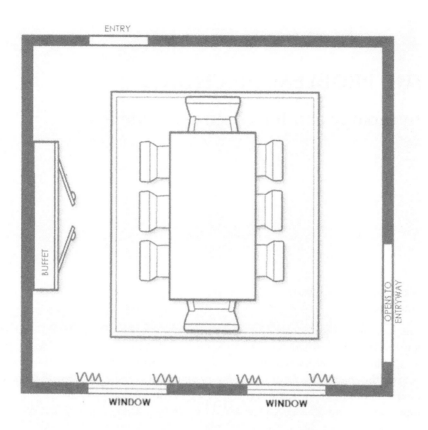

FIGURE 1.1 Geography example.

are throwing glances around the place willy-nilly ... and the audience would have no clear idea what is going or is looking at whom – they will not know the geography of the room.

Filmmakers mess with the geography of a scene at their own peril, because if something confuses the audience, you risk losing them and having them disengage from the story.

Now, knowing the importance of that, back to the director and their lunch ...

Our director had thoroughly prepared to establish good geography in order to cleanly execute a dramatic but complicated conclusion to their film; they had their storyboards and a birds-eye view map that diagrammed out the action that would take one character to safety through a labyrinth of cars locked in an accident pile-up caused by someone high up shooting at them. (This was indeed a very intense independent film.) And central to the geography was ...

FIGURE 1.2 Truck image.

... a metallic blue pickup truck so impressive everything in the scene's action had been designed around it. The director had fallen in love with it and designed their shots to make it the key to letting the audience know when the running character had reached a point of safety from the bullets fired from above. They were prepared with the best and – in their mind – the only way the final scene could be pulled off.

So everyone was feeling good as they took their final lunch break. Afterwards they'd get to the more important stuff: the runner weaving through the cars, working his way toward that blue truck, which would prove to be his salvation.

But then, at a late lunch meeting where the directory of photography (DP) and assistant director (AD) typically huddled to wolf down lunch while getting set for the rest of the day's shooting, disaster struck. It was during this rare moment of almost-relaxation, the finish line nearly in sight, that the owner of the beautiful blue semi-monster truck walked up, curtly jutted his chin, and said the words that nearly made the director require the Heimlich maneuver: "Gotta go." And with that turned and walked back toward his truck.

The director has said often that they wished they could remember more vividly the exchange that immediately followed. But they do recall a series of staccato images with muffled sounds (protests trying to find a way around a chunk of chicken salad). The long and short of it was this: someone had incorrectly told the Blue Truck Driver he and his vehicle were only needed for a few hours, not the entire day, and he was determined to take his truck to watch a true monster truck event happening an hour away.

The director does recall trying at first to reason with the Blue Truck Driver to stay, then arguing with him, maybe even threatening him (with what, they have no recollection), and finally begging him to stay, just long enough to reconfigure the shotlist to account for the blue truck's sudden disappearance from the scene's geography … all to no avail. The Driver climbed up in his truck, fired it up, and stomped the accelerator, smoking those big tires and peeling on out in such a cinematic display that – even in their shock – the team wished cameras were rolling.

Then it was … gone.

Gone … just like all of the director's perfectly prepared plans that were absolutely essential for the climactic scene's success. Gone … maybe just like any future potential career as a filmmaker!

The producer and AD ran over, turning from the settling smoke of burned rubber to the director's slack-jawed face and asking, "What are you going to do now?" Because here's the thing about shooting a film – it never stops. It's like the proverbial shark: once a production stops moving, it dies.

There are two warring adversaries constantly besieging a director, especially on an independent film: **time and money**. There's never enough of either. Maybe on a studio shoot with deeper pockets you could buy more time and say, "Okay, that's a wrap for today. Let's go back to the office and figure out how we're gonna deal with this armpit of a situation and restage and reshoot the entire scene tomorrow." But this wasn't a studio film; the director didn't have the luxury of losing a half day of shooting – there was a hard "out," as the crew like to say, meaning the end of the shoot; at the end of that day's shooting they were scheduled to wrap, and everyone would travel hours away back to home – and new jobs – the next day. *(Quick editorial aside here: don't schedule your most important scene for the final day of shooting – too many things can go wrong!)* So there wasn't the luxury of adding another day to the schedule to make up for this mistake – there was only now. The meter was ticking, the clock was ticking, and even the amount of daylight was ticking with the sun looking down saying, "You know I don't do overtime, right?"

And so once more, the producer repeated, "What are you doing to do now?"

A first impulse may be, "Lay down in the middle of this road right now, crawl into a ball and cry my eyes out!" But that couldn't happen, that wouldn't get anyone where they wanted to be. And where this director wanted to be was the head of a finished film with a kickass climactic sequence. And that meant they had to act *now* to make it happen – without the beautiful metallic pickup truck. Without the shotlist they had so carefully cultivated. Without all the options they thought would be available.

But that's when it happened, while they were standing in the middle of a country road with time, money and sun all ticking away and producers, cast and crew staring at them – **Clarity.**

To this day, our director can still feel this wave of utter calmness that suddenly blanketed their rising panic, much like a chemical fire suppressant dampens a fire. It was a defining moment, the kind sages, artists, and philosophers – and, possibly, one or two therapists – describe as how stripping away the veil of expectations can reveal the glow of possibilities. When options thought so important were instantly jerked away, the director inner's sight took hold, and they were forced to see what real choices remained. And the surprising thing was that they instantly knew what they saw was **better.** Why? Let's discuss.

The director had been so obsessed with this beautiful beast of a truck that they'd unconsciously started giving it more importance than the dramatic human elements. In all their perfect planning, they had made the classic directing mistake of highlighting a shining bauble – whether it be a vehicle, effect, stunt, prop, location, etc.—to the detriment of the characters and their story. Forced to come up with a new shooting plan that did not include the truck, the director almost instantly realized they had to re-balance the shotlist to focus on the interaction of the runner and the shooter.

The exact details of what happened next are slippery; all they recall is some kind of elemental creative force surged up, took over, and they immediately said, "The shotlist is scrapped – instead, here's what we're going to do now" … and then laid it out for everyone and did it. The cast and crew pitched right in, worked extra hard and fast, and as the last rays of sun slipped away that day, they had it: a finale that better accentuated the true dramatic needs of the scene.

And at the end of that day, after the production had wrapped the last shot of the film, our director stood on that narrow country road … and bawled their eyes out. Most of it was sheer exhaustion, some of it was a sadness that this special moment in their life – filming their directorial debut – was over … but definitely some of it was realizing how close they had come to shooting their climactic sequence from the ***wrong perspective***.

No one remembers anymore what the original shooting plan was; that shotlist may be buried somewhere in a binder in a storage locker, but it's no longer taking up any mental space. Now there is only the new, improvised approach, signaled by a tight close-up of the runner running into frame and stopping and realizing – much like his director – that the route he thought existed is not going to work and he needs to change course. That shot heralds the beginning of a better climactic sequence that didn't exist the morning of that shoot but revealed itself when options were taken away and choices clarified.

Oh, and the runner? Don't worry – he made it. And so will you.

Pt 2: **50 Flavors Meltdown**

Looking at that scenario, there was a real danger of the director losing the ***story*** – and at the end of the day, that is what we strive to create – original and impactful stories. As filmmakers, we should always be asking ourselves "does this serve the purpose of what I want to achieve with this film" – whether "this" be equipment, genre, cast, you name it. The director of the above example faced a moment of extreme adversity, but because of their knowledge of the story they wanted to tell they were able to finally realize not only could they reimagine their ending but, importantly, they should. However, that realization wasn't presented until an initial choice had been removed and negated. So how did the director come to a moment of clarity after a moment of serious chaos? Was it simply luck?

As we'll learn below, it was, of course, much more than that.

But first, this necessitates a quick discussion of what psychologists often refer to as the "problem of choice," which is an actual psychological phenomenon. This occurs when we are presented with so many options, that if we aren't prepared with either knowledge or experience, the result can actually be almost paralyzing rather than helpful.

The job of being a filmmaker is a challenging one. On the one hand, we want to learn as much as we can to make the best films we can. But today, as we walk through this journey together, we'll go over the little discussed flip side to that task – which is keeping a close eye on *how much* information we are learning at one time. This can have a direct and lasting effect on being able to differentiate amongst not only necessary but appropriate toolsets, ultimately leading to the best-told stories for any given situation. But before we begin to get into the nitty gritty, what exactly is the problem of choice in detail? Allow me to set the scene, dear reader.

Your friend asks you if you'd like to go get some ice cream. Sounds like a great plan! You are a major fan of mint chocolate chip in particular. They tell you there's a fantastic new store that has not 5, not 15, but 50 ice cream flavors. Well 50 sounds a lot better than 5! So many options! Then, the two of you enter the store, and you realize you are totally frozen (if you will). And you find yourself staring at 50 different kinds of dessert options. Suddenly, while you initially thought the mint chocolate chip would be fantastic, it's now entirely possible that blueberry cheesecake just *might* be better. What to do?

This scenario is not unlike a very famous "Jam" study, where in two separate scenarios, customers could choose from a small number of different flavors of jams, or a much broader but therefore unfamiliar array of flavors. Consistently, customers felt much more confident in the decision made from the *limited* jam options. (There's that word again: limited.) Why? Because there was less room for doubt, and – in what will become key for us – a greater understanding of the available options.

The overwhelming scenario of options can be incapacitating in general, but especially so to those who do not know what they're looking for yet. And one of the elements that's so overlooked is the fact that in learning new techniques and skillsets, it's entirely possible we try to learn *too much* at once. Particularly, in the art of filmmaking we have many, many storytelling elements at our disposal. These include, but are not limited to

- Genres
- Story structure
- Length
- Resources (equipment, funds, etc.)
- Blocking/shooting of scenes

The list goes on.

It's not enough to simply say that having too many options in and of itself is bad; how do you even know when you've reached *too* much, and therefore the *full capabilities of what you have left*? The trick here is it can be hard to tell, especially early in your career, what the entire potential of each tool is before you may be put in a position to ultimately have to choose between many items of equipment, many genre options, and therefore modes of storytelling. Often, you are taking classes regarding production *and* storytelling simultaneously that present all-or-nothing models rather than thin slices that fully examine a particular mode of expression. Adding to that, filmmaking is a tightrope stretched between the demands of right-brained (creativity, imagination, etc.) and left-brained (logistics, linear thinking, etc.) thinking – filmmakers often have to balance the creative needs of storytelling with the cruel logistics of budgeting and scheduling a shoot. The pushme-pullyou of this schism can add to the overwhelm when one is confronted by all the choices that must be made.

All of this ultimately leads us here today to a goal of providing clarity of choice in the creative process for you – building a clean reference for skillsets and available storytelling tools. And it is this concise and clear understanding that will enable you to not only examine the best elements to tell your story but, much like the director's original scenario that kicked off this chapter, what to do when presented with adverse situations that can be more clearly recognized as opportunities, given the right knowledge and experience. Minus the near panic attack, of course. Because until you learn what you can really do with what you already have, you won't realize all you truly have.

Through both historical context as well as contemporary examples, and specific exercises to strengthen filmmaking muscles, we'll parse that knowledge and transform it into real-life experience. By momentarily limiting choices to better learn the full capabilities of each option you may be presented with, you'll be able to move forward viewing possible restrictions not as liabilities, but as opportunities for creative thought and productive workflow. Should you choose to accept this mission – read on!

2
HISTORICAL LIMITATIONS THROUGHOUT FILM PRODUCTION'S EVOLUTION LEADING TO INNOVATION

Throughout history, cinema has consistently evolved from the discovery of the photochemical process to the digital pixel, to the extensive range of viewing formats that we witness today. The ebb and flow and the mechanics of how and why different evolutions have taken place are fascinating and nuanced. Not least fascinating of these are certain movements derived from profound periods or instances of distinct situations of limitations – some rather unexpected. While we cannot delve into all of these happenings in exceptional depth, for each instance we discuss here, we will touch on these very important moments in cinema's history in which pronounced limitations – either outwardly enforced, technically evolutionary, economically stifling or otherwise – directly impacted the manner in which we tell stories. And we will discuss what came out on the other side, and why that matters to us as storytellers today. From innovations that arose out of the unexpected limitations that developed with the advent of sound to those created by the inevitable impact of the World Wars, these foundational movements are pivotal to an understanding of the definition of innovation through creative limitations and some amazing examples of the ways that art advanced and expanded as it continued expressive evolution amidst adversity.

2.1 World Wars, Isolation, and Storytelling
2.1.1 What It Was

The World Wars, perhaps more than any other large-scale occurrence, can be pinpointed as the source or catalyst for many major art movements of our time. When we take a step back and truly examine the work we have been immersed in, not merely in cinema, but especially in one of its major precursors – painting – the impact is profound and global in scale. The massive catastrophes and rerouting of communities and entire cities, the extraordinary loss, and subsequent effect on all citizens, are immense and of extraordinary humanitarian impact.

The work of individual artists has been known to dramatically change over the course of a singular lifetime during and after a war, and its effects cannot be overstated with regard to the potential of altering entire methods of expression.

Examining the artistic replies that occurred due to human responses to tragedies, the attitude that we are taking at this moment is simply that this is what it was – not that the source of the movement was in any way desirable. Thinking of Hollywood's Red Scare for example – a direct result of the fear of Communism and the Cold War fears brewing between the then Soviet Union and United States in the 1940s and 1950s most specifically, films such as *On The Waterfront* were eventually produced, which taken objectively are examples of great screenwriting and allegories of creating pariahs of other human beings – but one has to take a step back and wonder, should this situation have happened in the first place to cause someone to feel the feelings that created these works – on either side? That particular film leaves a to-this-day lingering feeling of frost in the air, as both its director Elia Kazaan and screenwriter Budd Schulberg had testified and "named names" of fellow artists they at least verbally felt were of undue communist influence, in front of the House UnAmerican Activities Committee (HUAC) during Hollywood's terrible Blacklist period of the 1950s. The HUAC sought to find, humiliate, and degrade those who had affiliations with or undue influence by Communists,[1] and as a result, many cinematic artists of all kinds were essentially blacklisted from working in Hollywood – at least by their known names.

So what do we make of works that stem from such difficult moments, and from times and situations that are, to put it *lightly, unideal*?

These are difficult questions, so we present these events and their subsequent impact on artists and movements here in ways illuminating that through extraordinarily challenging times, there are glimpses of work that despite all odds speak truth and innovate – seemingly when it would seem impossible. Often the source of inspiration isn't very calm. Often, it's not very pretty and can be a source of great struggle.

And so what we will examine to really understand this because to fully take a look at the ebb and flow of Art movements and responses to the Wars in full is its own book - is one specific example in Cinema that impacts us to this day – German Expressionism. German Expressionism was caused fairly directly by a decision made after the end of the World War I, and the economic hardships faced by a country reeling from battle, now left to handle both reparations and economic isolationism.

2.1.2 Background: Art + World War I

With the 1914 assassination of Austro-Hungarian Archduke Ferdinand, a chain reaction ignites that begins the largest war the world has seen to that point – lasting four years, involving 25 countries, and costing 9 million lives.[2]

Prior to the outbreak of World War I, the world was on the precipice of breakthroughs in industrialization and mechanical engineering, and as a result, there was a rise in nationalistic tendencies in many countries. These themes were present in art as well, with works expressing themselves in the dramatic, bold lines of the Futurists and Cubists. These movements would later be rejected as artists were severely impacted by their experiences of grief, trauma, and loss during the war.

FIGURE 2.1 *Unique Forms of Continuity in Space,* 1913 bronze by Umberto Boccioni – Futurism.

What we begin to see take shape are Dadaism and Surrealism as the strongest aesthetic reactions arising from World War I – this in stark contrast and as a seeming rebuttal to the more mechanical and hard lined Futurism and Cubism. From the Tate's "Nine Ways Artists Responded to the First World War," –

> Unable to comprehend the harsh realities of war, artists began looking at more unconventional ways to express themselves. The founders of the surrealist

movement, André Breton and Louis Aragon, had been medical students at a military hospital in Paris in 1917. They had been eyewitnesses to the horror of the war and how this had damaged the bodies of its victims. While an effort was made by artists like Henry Tonks to document the wounds soldiers had experienced, the surrealists felt these articles were unable to fully realize the horror of the experience.

FIGURE 2.2 Marcel Duchamp *Fountain*, 1917, photograph by Alfred Stieglitz at 291 art gallery following the 1917 Society of Independent Artists exhibit, with entry tag visible. The backdrop is *The Warriors* by Marsden Hartley.

The German Max Ernst was a key artist working within the surrealist movement. His *Celebes* presents a fragmented body and a tank, elephant-like in stature. Ernst explores the distorted post-war psyche, affected by shellshock and trauma. The suggested meaning is that the individual, notably female, is helpless against the might of the machine. Confused and disorientated, artists began to make art that posed more questions than it answered.

Likewise, the dada movement that began in Zurich was a direct reaction to the war. It subverted traditional ideas and satirized war rhetoric. Kurt Schwitters's artwork takes ideas from both dada and surrealism and presents a fragmented vision of a post-war society. His *Picture of Spatial Growths – Picture with Two Small Dogs* is a collage of rubbish and printed ephemera from Germany in 1920. He added to the piece 17 years later, creating various layers. Its collage form creates a messiness and disorder that relates to the struggling and bankrupt Weimar Germany Schwitters was working in.[3]

Following the denouement, at the 1919 Treaty of Versailles Germany was held responsible for actions that began the war. As a result, there are severe sanctions, loss of territory, and demilitarization penalties embedded within the document. The economic sanctions are so severe in fact, there was no way that the country would ever be able to pay them without total economic collapse. The effect of this, the inability to have a military, to trade, and the subsequent severe isolation this causes, would stir up extreme nationalism fostering groups that include the Nazi party, who take the stage as we head into World War II.

2.1.3 Innovative Case Study: German Expressionism + The Cabinet of Dr. Caligari, 1920

We're going to pause to discuss something that occurred during this intermediary period of Isolation – a moment of Art Expression that was so interesting and dramatic, that it still affects us to this day. That movement was called **German Expressionism,** and one of its greatest works in cinema was *The Cabinet of Dr. Caligari* directed by Robert Wiene.

As a degree of background, after World War I begins in 1914, Germany banned all foreign film titles in 1916. And there cannot simply not be films for the public. So there is a desire for increased local productions. This aids the elevation of directors such as R.W. Murnaur and Fritz Lang, both of whom explore themes of violence, and darkness in much of their work. German Expressionism itself was not new to Cinema and in fact had been seen (as often happens) in painting prior. Elements typical of the movement included -

> Bright and vivid colors, sweeping brushstrokes, bold markings and basic forms came together to create compositions that reflected emotion and expression. Artists interpreted reality through the lens of their own inner thoughts and feelings, providing a platform for audiences to explore the events happening around them in a deeper way. In turn, this encouraged audiences to expand their views of art as well. Films such as *The Cabinet of Dr. Caligari* drew upon themes of reality, such as a soldier's experience in World War I and the reality of a new social and political structure. A wariness of authoritarian leadership underpinned

the themes of horror and dramatic distortions of sets, costumes, and props. Lighting was a critical element in capturing Expressionism on film—shadows and angular portrayals mirrored the statements made by brushstrokes and color in German Expressionist paintings. To this day, filmmakers such as Tim Burton and M. Night Shyamalan have drawn inspiration from the dramatic renderings of German Expressionism in film.[4]

FIGURE 2.3 *Cabinet of Dr Caligari* 1920 Lobby Card.

In the film, the evil Doctor Caligari uses a Somnambulist to commit atrocities upon townspeople at night, with the vivid sets painted with the gorgeous expressionist severity typical of the movement. It should also be noted that at times economics were so severely dire, that lighting patterns and shadows could earnestly be painted on the set, the cinematic moods were so bombastic that this was another way of saving money during the crisis. The makeup, costume design, dark plotlines, and overall emotional fortitude of the piece are all emblematic not just of the Expressionist movement itself, but of a country that was experiencing a very extraordinary period of isolation, of economic hardship, and was about to hurdle onward into full-on nationalism preceding World War II.

To conclude, visual approach and severe economic restrictions led to decision making in artistic studios that hadn't been attempted before. There were new aesthetics taking place in coordination with lensing and framing in narrative structure, causing innovation in dramatic storytelling that we still see today throughout many genres. We observed the nouveau establishment of art movements – in film specifically we have Dadaists, Surrealists, and Expressionists as well as an aesthetic evolution spawned through severe economic restriction and propaganda dissemination, as well as entire genre evolutions dictated by isolationism and reparations.

2.2 Pre-Sound to Post-Sound

Short of the formation of the photographic image, arguably there was no bigger moment in cinematic discoveries than that of the alignment of synched sound to the moving picture image. This new technological approach to storytelling completely altered the way in which we were experiencing narrative, absorbing information in front of and around us in the theater, and also changing the nature of the physical theater itself.

Prior to the advent of sound, films were not watched in silence, though – they were actively and audibly taken in by an audience who sat in front of a screen that was flanked by an orchestra, which would accompany the piece with music and sound compliments designed to emphasize and further characterize the film's tones and themes.

Film was unfortunately beginning to really innovate in terms of the integration of the grammar and language of the shot and editing sequences developed in linear cinema language to tell stories. It's often said that if sound had simply waited even 10 more years, we'd be light years ahead of where we are now visually. Artists such as Buster Keaton were mastering choreographed movements in line with action sequences, while Dorothy Azner innovated editing techniques that were nimble enough to carry over across the multiple genres she was asked to direct.[5]

However in 1927, with the line "Wait a minute, wait a minute. You ain't seen nothin' yet!" Al Jolson controversially launched the "popular" film scene into the sound world, never to be the same again – both from a storytelling perspective and the way we physically experience cinema. Controversially is used here to acknowledge that Jolson was utilizing the extremely problematic use of blackface in the film *The Jazz Singer*. The use of blackface was not only shamefully harmful in its prejudicial representation of Black Americans, but it also by simply being allowed onscreen, stopped Black actors from being able to act in roles as well. So for every moment of progress, there are unfortunately moments of serious issues – here prejudice and racial disparity. Technology was moving right along, but humanity was, per usual, having a lot of concerning moments. That needs to be acknowledged because Jolson is regarded very widely as a problematic cinematic persona – though he is the person who is known for introducing sound to a "popular" audience.

"Popular" above is in quotes because while 1927 became the year that sound more broadly became a larger trend in filmmaking, efforts to incorporate it alongside the moving image had been going on for some time. These efforts (dating back to 1894 if you can believe it, with the *Dickson Experimental Sound Film*) couldn't effectively meld the existing sound technology of the time into the rapidly progressing visual medium that was the moving picture image, and its expanding grammar of shots and story language.[6] Technology hadn't caught up yet to a point where the recording and synching of the sound in real time, could be accomplished in a manner not cumbersome to being incorporated into the medium. However by the early 1920s, studios had invested in recording technology, which after trial and error with items such as Phonofilm, got to a point of workability with the Vitaphone – of which many films had been recorded onto prior to *The Jazz Singer*, it should be noted. The Vitaphone was an almost record-like device that could play sound for approximately 10–11 minutes and was used for orchestral or sound effects play-back initially. The reason *The Jazz Singer* became noteworthy in addition to its intentional use of (at the time) bankable stars in a "sound" film, was its use of synched dialogue on the Vitaphone's playback system. To hear the voice in real time of the screen stars at that time – that was quite something.

So what exactly was the impact of sound on film?

With regards to the latter, there were many jobs created when we now have an entirely new sense to fulfill within the world of the film – on set, in pre- and post-production. But there were also many jobs lost of those who were creating the sound we don't speak often about or even learn about – those in the theater on instruments creating the scores and sonic, live experiences that were happening in early cinema works. Not only that, many actors who simply could not adapt to the differences of form that sound introduced – subtleties of movement, tone of voice (the epically satirized Lena in *Singing in the Rain* comes to mind), simply could no longer continue. A wonderful exception, Lillian Gish – one of the screen's most notable early actors, found consistent work throughout her career as the manner and technique of film production changed and required very different techniques and adaptive approaches from its actors. Gish was also gifted as a theater actor, and able to transcend film's movement into the sound age, though she remained a strong advocate for silent films later on.[7]

2.2.1 Why was This A Moment of Innovation

- **Changing of Shot length, and Therefore of Language**

Dialogue completely changed the duration and dictation of how shots were cut. Prior, we were relying primarily on body language to tell our stories, which were plot-driven, but primarily in an action sense, with minimal dialogue, whittled down to occasional title cards.

- **Screenwriting Emerges as a Fully Formed Artform**

Prior to the necessity of real-time dialogue, the Screenwriter wasn't necessarily an active, paid position in the film world. Stories were developed in coordination with the director, producer, cinematographer and studio heads; however, the active role of the writer and the evolution of dialogue itself completely changed (and obviously so) after the arrival of the synched word.

- **Film moves more Fully Away from Theater**

Film begins to encompass final, fully fleshed-out works that are consistent for each viewing as opposed to those with an orchestral accompaniment.

- **Film Acting Changes**

Initially incredibly stilted as the design of microphones catches up and engages with cameras that were not designed for sound, the artform evolves once again and in this regard continues its path away from the stage's craft ever more definitively.

2.2.2 Innovative Case Study: Dorothy Arzner's The Wild Party (1929), and The Invention of the Boom Pole and Shotgun Microphone

Growing up with a sufficient background in film production, Dorothy Arzner is considered not just one of the most successful female directors of the early 20th century, but also notably one who successfully made a transition from silent work to sound pictures. After early work as a screenplay typist and film editor, it was her tenacity and competency for on-budget, successful productions and her ability to masterfully move from pre- to post-production that enabled her to find success in a field dominated by men. Notable early silent works included films such as *Old Ironsides* (1926), *Get Your Man* (1927), and *Manhattan Cockatil* (1928).[8]

But it was her 1929 "Talkie" *The Wild Party* about a group of young women who prefer parties over their studies, that is the focus of our example. In the film, former silent film actor Clara Bow in her first talking picture, plays Stella – a young college student who falls for an Anthropology professor who isn't thrilled with her hard partying. Of interest for us, was the innovative use of technology that Arzner developed in response to Bow's adaptations to the sound film's different acting requirements and physicality. With microphone technology still so new, there was not the lavalier microphone and freedom of movement that we currently see on set today. In fact, often actors who had formerly enjoyed extensive movement in their silent film frames were forced to stay relatively still in order for a microphone – often placed in a vase or set of flowers – to cleanly pick up their audio. As Maria Lewis mentions in her brilliant write up on Arzner for ACMI,

> So successful were her features at Paramount, she was barely in her 30s when the studio tasked her with making their first 'talkie': *The Wild Party* (1929). Besides being a significant commercial hit – and spawning a sub-genre of comedies about hard-partying college students – it was crucial to the invention of the boom mic. With silent movie star Clara Bow in the lead role, the actress was struggling with her physical performance due to the need to stay still so the on-set microphone could pick up her audio. Arzner came up with the idea to rig a microphone to a fishing rod and have technicians lower it over Bow's head, so she wouldn't be restricted. It's a device more commonly known as the boom mic today and the concept was patented shortly after.[9]

Historical Limitations Throughout Film Production's **19**

FIGURE 2.4 Clara Bow and Dorothy Arzner on the set of *The Wild Party*, 1929.

Once again, we see adaptation arriving with a permanent - and in this case massive - impact to cinema's development, out of sheer necessity and lack of appropriate resources.

2.3 The Hays Code and Cinema Censorship

2.3.1 What It Was

We completely understand where you're coming from right now – how can censorship in any way lead to innovation? And we're so glad you are asking! But often it's not until we are at our minimum allowances that we find what we are truly capable of. Are Bill and Ingrid telling you to go out and deliberately put the following restrictions on yourself? Oh gosh, no! But here's the moral of this section's story – if these artists can make work through these guidelines, we have a gut feeling you might just be ok!

In order to understand the Hays code and the context in which this set of rules was established and why, we need to take things back to the roaring 20s – and the subsequent hit of the Great Depression.

Following a period of incredible progress and change during the 1920s, during which time we had the evolution of Aviation, the ending of the first World War, the onset of synched dialogue in film (heyo!), the new musical style to become known as Jazz, our first Radio Broadcast from Ingrid's hometown of Pittsburgh, Pennsylvania, and a swathe of progressive movement forward, these exciting leaps enabled many people to perhaps all too optimistically believe or expect there was an economic cushion available, and that life was good – *very* good. But unfortunately, things were not to stay quite so good for very long …

And in 1929, the Wall Street crash suddenly but effectively ended what had become known as *The Jazz Age*.

FIGURE 2.5 1920 Unemployed men queued outside a depression soup kitchen opened in Chicago by Al Capone.

What was that crashing sound, you ask? Let's discuss. The Stock Market, the center of the New York City Stock Exchange, collapsed in October of 1929. To have an understanding of what was essentially happening to cause this, you had investors buying stock (or portions of companies available for sale) for more than its actual value, oftentimes with borrowed money (or "on margin"), because at the time – once again – the era was booming, and there was a feeling that you couldn't go wrong. Except simultaneously something else was also happening. There were beginnings of excessive droughts causing a rise in food prices due to shortages. This had an impact on national labor availability, which then caused layoffs. Banks began to have an inability to consistently liquidate larger and larger loans that were being requested from their clientele. And these pressures began to squeeze the national economic food chain, causing investors in the Stock Market to feel the need to "dump" their shares so to speak, or trade them – leading to two famously terrible days of massive and rapid Stock Trades - Black Thursday (24 October 1929), and the following Black Tuesday (29 October 1929).

The rapid trading of the stocks epically lessened their value, causing investors to lose at times all of their money (not to mention other peoples' money), and the national market to go into free fall. This exacerbated the already stewing economic situation, and was a massive contributor to the Great Depression's subsequent decade in which Herbert Hoover – whose belief that the national government should be hands-off in economics – would be replaced by Franklin Deleno Roosevelt, whose work with The New Deal as well as the removal of the United States from the global monetary Gold Standard would step by step pull the country to the precipice of exiting the Depression. That is until we reached the edge of World War I and the necessity of industrialized jobs for the creation of its war machines.[10]

That's a lot of background but it's super important for us, so you feel like you've got it? Wonderful. Now – to the Hays Code! During the Great Depression, no one had the money to invest any more in Cinema.

FIGURE 2.6 1920 American Union Bank.

For heaven's sake, there were bigger fish to fry! So to get people into the theater, studio heads had to think creatively, and frankly that might mean getting a bit … risqué. Themes at the time bordered on the garish and grotesque, or sometimes veered into more tawdry elements very deliberately knowing that this would attract a crowd. There were certainly gestures and overtures designed to titillate and draw the dollar, because frankly there weren't many dollars to draw! And this also was on the tails of the 1920s, which was an extremely liberated decade comparatively. Films were therefore very progressive and explorative – with women and openly queer directors making works that pushed boundaries, *particularly* before the advent of sound. We had momentarily an increased building of very bold storylines, not simply out of an evolution of creative expression, but also, to be frank, we had to get some butts in the seats to sell tickets![11]

So what exactly *is* the Hays Code and why talk about it? Keeping in mind the timing of this was also impacted by the fact that we are coming out of a World War, the Hays code is named after William H Hays, the President of the Motion Picture Producers and Distributors of America, and it is a

> self-imposed industry set of guidelines for all the motion pictures that were released between 1934 and 1968. The code prohibited profanity, suggestive nudity, graphic or realistic violence, sexual persuasions and rape. It had rules around the use of crime, costume, dance, religion, national sentiment and morality. And according to the code – even within the limits of pure love or realistic love – certain facts have been regarded as outside the limits of safe presentation.[12]

Now, who *was* William H. Hays? Let's get to it because this is a bit interesting when you pause to think about who was at the helm of dictating cinematic storytelling rules alongside the Catholic League of America for 30 years.

FIGURE 2.7 William Harrison Hays.

William Hays was originally a manager of Warren G. Harding's Presidential campaign. A Conservative Republican, he then was subsequently appointed to the role of Postmaster General of the United States. But shortly afterwards he became the head of Hollywood's Motion Picture Producer and Distributors of America – later to become The Motion Picture Association of America. When he took the role, the goal of the organization was essentially to clean up the motion picture industry, following numerous scandals of the 1920s, including one involving notable movie star Fatty Arbuckle's alleged involvement in a murder and possible rape.

Importantly, Hays initially came up with a list of 11 absolute "do nots" and 25 slightly looser "be very careful's;" however, these were ultimately short lived, as sound would change everything about what would theoretically need to be censored. And in 1931, we get the Motion Picture Production Code, also known as ... The Hays Code. Initially, the Hays Code didn't have a lot of weight in the Motion Picture industry, in fact initially no one particularly followed its guidelines or felt much pressure to be bound by any repercussions.

Once again with Maria Lewis,

> Filmmakers such as Dorothy Arzner, who continued the legacy of female film pioneers like Lois Weber, continued to push the conservative boundaries of the new Hays Hollywood. As an openly queer filmmaker and the only female director active during Hollywood's Golden Age, she made openly feminist films like the first talkie directed by a woman, *The Wild Party* (1929), and *Dance, Girl, Dance* (1940), the latter a "Code-stretching" tale of burlesque dancers that challenges the male gaze (and audiences). In fact, as talkies began to take over as the preferred format among audiences in the late 1920s, progressive stories were still slipping through the cracks until the mid-30s as the code was rarely enforced.[13]

But when backed by the subsequent Legion of Decency – a group of Jewish and Protestant organizations who decided to publicly boycott films they deemed as indecent – things began to take shape. Films couldn't afford to lose money to boycotts from religious organizations, and the Hays office set up The Production Code Administration (PCA). The PCA was given the authority not just to edit out morally objectionable material from original scripts, but ultimately from final cuts as well.

What were the guidelines you ask? So glad you did, dear reader! Below are the Motion Picture Production Code principles – and please, take your time!

2.3.2 General Principles

1 No picture shall be produced which will lower the moral standards of those who see it. Hence the sympathy of the audience should never be thrown to the side of crime, wrongdoing, evil, or sin.

2 Correct standards of life, subject only to the requirements of drama and entertainment, shall be presented.

3 Law, natural or human, shall not be ridiculed, nor shall sympathy be created for its violation.

2.3.3 Particular Applications

I **Crimes Against the Law**
These shall never be presented in such a way as to throw sympathy with the crime as against law and justice or to inspire others with a desire for imitation.

1 *Murder*
   a The technique of murder must be presented in a way that will not inspire imitation.
   b Brutal killings are not to be presented in detail.
   c Revenge in modern times shall not be justified.

2 *Methods of Crime* should not be explicitly presented.
   a Theft, robbery, safe-cracking, and dynamiting of trains, mines, buildings, etc., should not be detailed in method.
   b Arson must be subject to the same safeguards.
   c The use of firearms should be restricted to essentials.
   d Methods of smuggling should not be presented.

3 *Illegal drug traffic* must never be presented.

4 *The use of liquor* in American life, when not required by the plot or for proper characterization will not be shown.

II **Sex**
The sanctity of the institution of marriage and the home shall be upheld. Pictures shall not infer that low forms of sex relationship are the accepted or common thing.

1 *Adultery,* sometimes necessary plot material, must not be explicitly treated, or justified, or presented attractively.

2 *Scenes of Passion*
   a They should not be introduced when not essential to the plot.

b Excessive and lustful kissing, lustful embraces, suggestive postures and gestures, are not to be shown.
   c In general, passion should so be treated that these scenes do not stimulate the lower and baser element.

3 *Seduction or Rape*
   a They should never be more than suggested, and only when essential for the plot, and even then never shown by explicit method.
   b They are never the proper subject for comedy.

4 *Sex perversion* or any inference to it is forbidden.

5 *White-slavery* shall not be treated.

6 *Miscegenation* (sex relationships between the white and black races) is forbidden.

7 *Sex hygiene* and venereal diseases are not subjects for motion pictures.

8 Scenes of *actual child birth,* in fact or in silhouette, are never to be presented.

9 *Children's sex organs* are never to be exposed.

III Vulgarity
The treatment of low, disgusting, unpleasant, though not necessarily evil, subjects should be subject always to the dictates of good taste and a regard for the sensibilities of the audience.

IV Obscenity
Obscenity in word, gesture, reference, song, joke, or by suggestion (even when likely to be understood only by part of the audience) is forbidden.

V Profanity
Pointed profanity (this includes the words, God, Lord, Jesus, Christ – unless used reverently – Hell, S.O.B. damn, Gawd), or every other profane or vulgar expression, however used, is forbidden.

VI Costume
1 *Complete nudity* is never permitted. This includes nudity in fact or in silhouette, or any lecherous or licentious notice thereof by other characters in the picture.
2 *Undressing scenes* should be avoided, and never used save where essential to the plot.
3 *Indecent or undue exposure* is forbidden.
4 *Dancing costumes* intended to permit undue exposure or indecent movements in the dance are forbidden.

VII **Dances**

1 Dances suggesting or representing sexual actions or indecent passion are forbidden.
2 Dances that emphasize indecent movements are to be regarded as obscene.

VIII **Religion**

1 No film or episode may throw ridicule on any religious faith.
2 *Ministers of religion* in their character as ministers of religion should not be used as comic characters or as villains.
3 *Ceremonies* of any definite religion should be carefully and respectfully handled.

IX **Locations**

The treatment of bedrooms must be governed by good taste and delicacy.

X **National Feelings**

1 *The use of the Flag* shall be consistently respectful.
2 *The history,* institutions, prominent people, and citizenry of other nations shall be represented fairly.

XI **Titles**

Salacious, indecent, or obscene titles shall not be used.

XII **Repellent Subjects**

The following subjects must be treated within the careful limits of good taste:

1 *Actual hangings* or electrocutions as legal punishments for crime.
2 *Third Degree* methods.
3 *Brutality* and possible gruesomeness.
4 *Branding* of people or animals.
5 *Apparent cruelty* to children or animals.
6 *The sale of women* or a woman selling her virtue.
7 *Surgical operations.*[14]

Sheesh! Seems like a lot to follow, doesn't it? Well, the pendulum swung both ways, and there are reports that sometimes directors and screenwriters found it a bit of a relief in terms of their development process to simply know where their storylines were going to end up. At the other end of the spectrum, you have infamous examples like Howard Hughes who fought tooth and nail to get his original edit of 1931's *Scarface* to the screen.[15]

Eventually, in 1968, we moved towards the Jack Asner Movie Ratings System as the code ultimately continued to lose credibility and meaning, and public favor and opinion of films released in independently owned theaters, create national hits of works that defy PCA codes of conduct. The initial Asner ratings system you may find familiar – it was of course:

G(eneral audiences)
M(ature audiences)
R(restricted)
X(Adults only)

This eventually evolves in the 1980's to:

G(eneral audiences)
PG (General public)
PG-13
R(restricted)
NC-17(Over the age of 17)

2.3.4 Why Was This A Moment of Innovation:

- **Essentially in many aspects stories had to be told in an entirely different way**

That could take the form of screenwriting, shot angles, final edits, scene approaches, you name it. What you did or did not see on screen was paramount, and a decision that was made ever more important during this period, as opposed to our earlier cinematic moments in narrative, particularly as we were moving away from the artform of early Theater and Vaudeville, in which elements were much more performative and at times quite literal and lengthier in their approach. The Hays Code in its way forced filmmakers to decide what was vitally important, and what had to be onscreen, verses what could be alluded to in other ways – and who could pick up on them.

- **How Far is too far?**

In later years, as we will see below in our case study, it also posed an important question – how far will you be pushed? Billy Wilder reached his limits and knew he had a bankable set of stars, an amazing script, and a massive hit on his hands any way the chips fell. He ran with it, Hays Code be damned, and opened the door to the crumbling of this draconian censorship model that relied on religious authority and bullying to enforce its mandates, as he directed what many consider a penultimate comedic work.

28 Limitation Throughout History

2.3.5 Innovative Case Study: Some Like It Hot, 1959

FIGURE 2.8 *Some Like It Hot* (1959 theatrical poster).

Some LIke it Hot, the story of two prohibition-era Chicago musicians who witness the Saint Valentine's Day massacre and must escape by joining an all-girl band in 1929 Florida, while somewhat reliant on a 2-gender system of operation for the success of its humor, was an important work not simply in the protesting and ultimate demise of the Hays Code, but also in not forcing the art to bend any longer to the whims of an archaic system, by subverting its rules and quite simply being too clever to be stopped.

Moments of finding ways to get around the restriction in interesting capacities – costume, dialogue, and use of genre to essentially restrict violence categorization, were hugely integral to the film's success in undermining the system of censorship that had befallen so many other plotlines and storytelling devices of its film-making kin.

Billy Wilder and I.A.L. Diamond's screenplay, full of double entendres and innuendos that weren't technically literal and therefore elusive to the cut, were so cleverly written that while recognizable (and *funny*), they were often so quick to the punch that the Code would be genuinely hard pressed to pursue any one of them in detail.

Orry-Kelly's brilliantly sexy costumes in *Some Like It Hot* weren't actually revealing, but extraordinarily suggestive and gorgeous.

FIGURE 2.9 Some Like It Hot, 1959 with Tony Curtis, Jack Lemmon and Marilyn Monroe.

Kelly, one of the few openly gay costume designers at that time, established a beautiful career making gorgeous designs, at a time when being in a same-sex relationship could cost you your job, let alone working on a film putting two men in dresses:

> At that time, being in a same-sex relationship was a career-killer—it certainly ended the career of Billy Haines, a star of the silent and early sound eras, as he would not give in to studio demands that he leave his partner. And there were even more dire consequences for being gay, like being blackmailed or arrested. There was pressure on behind-the-scenes personnel as well. Top gay costume designers Travis Banton and the single-named Adrian yielded to it, entering into marriages of convenience … The closet meant job security. But the closet was not for Orry-Kelly, and he managed a stellar career just the same.[16]

He famously dressed actresses like Bette Davis (*Jezebel, Now Voyager*), and Ingrid Bergman (*Casablanca*), created dresses for Jack Lemmon, Tony Curtis, and Marilyn Monroe – all cut and bedazzled in just the right places to strongly suggest but never reveal exactly what was beneath. Orry-Kelly created the fantastical creations for Busby Berkley's musical numbers, and had a great familiarity with not simply how far to push the envelope, but when it would tear. He had a knack for integrating costumes with the stories as well as collaborating with his actors and actresses, and was an integral and vital element of the successes of these films.[17]

And the violence of the 1920s set gangsters – while as realistic as any other films of that time, were embedded technically within the confines of a comedy. So any way you sliced it, this film had a backup plan for any argument that may be coming its way from the PCA board. But you know what? They honestly didn't seem to care! *Some Like It Hot* was released to massive appeal and six Oscars (including Best Costume and Best Screenplay), and the Hays Code would ultimately begin to lose steam before its demise and evolution into the Motion Picture Ratings system in 1968.

2.4 Black and White Meets Color

2.4.1 What It Was

When we think of the transition of film from Black and White to color, we often don't realize how long the overall transition was that took place. This is an honest mistake as looking back at great films, sometimes it can be challenging when some from the very same year are both color *and* black and white. But the overall process from the time that color processes started to be introduced to the time that films fully came onboard actually took close to about 30 years – and not for reasons you may think. In fact, some of it wasn't even about technology even though that did take a second – don't get us wrong. So what's the deal with the evolution? Let's get a quick background before we go into why this was such a key time for innovation.

Early on, our first foray into the introduction of color arrived with the Technicolor subtractive process by Herbert Kalmus, which utilized red and green negative film overlaid on top of one another. The year was 1915. While used in several films during the 1920's such as Warner Bros *On With The Show!* the process's overall technology and printing capabilities weren't up to speed or coming in on budget, and so Technicolor then developed a Three-Strip Process, wonderfully described in Rachel Elfassy Bitoun's A History of Color: The Difficult Transition from Black & White Cinematography:

> In 1932, where two 35mm strips of black and white film negatives, one sensitive to blue and the other to red, ran together through an aperture behind a magenta filter. A separate strip allowed the green light to pass through behind a green filter. The lights were divided through a prism and refracted by mirrors through the different filters, all in a single camera.[18]

The three-strip process also required an excessive amount of light, often two or three times that of Black and White sets, and tales from films such as *The Wizard of Oz* are legend, with actors needing frequent water breaks, temperatures reaching above 38 degrees Celsius, and some actors reporting possible permanent eye damage (according to Richard. B. Jewell in *The Golden Age of Cinema*). The cameras were large and challenging to move, camera tricks were limited, and deep focus wasn't achievable. However, despite these challenges, Technicolor did boast achievements in the 1940s, particularly with films such as *Gone With the Wind,* which took home Academy Awards.

FIGURE 2.10 3 strip Technicolor camera, by Marcin Wichary from San Francisco, U.S.A. - Humble beginnings, pt. 5 MOMI.

Source: https://commons.wikimedia.org/wiki/File:3-strip_Technicolor_camera.jpg

It was another company though, Eastman Kodak, that would refine the ways in which color processing would ultimately find success in film. In 1952, the company introduced Eastmancolor, which was a single-strip color negative film. It was a game changer, so much so that the final Technicolor shoot took place just two years later, in 1954.

But even with the patent of Eastman Kodak, Black and White was still the norm, with the evolution of cinematography techniques and innovations to that point belonging to that aesthetic. People also didn't believe color could properly expose on film the way it presented to the eye in real life – and there wasn't convincing evidence initially that that would necessarily ever happen. Once again with Rachel Elfassy Bitoun,

> People assumed colour was incompatible with film's other practices and would therefore radically change the nature of cinema. Colour would also have an impact on human sight and health, and disrupt the audience's vision. Screen colour was apprehended in a total different form than human natural vision, and people did not believe that film could expose colour as we see it every day. Film director John Huston said that "colour in nature is very different from colour on screen" as it appeared too bright and too vivid. It lacked subtlety and definition, and did not provide natural effects, but instead "isolated objects with an effect of verisimilitude" and gave birth to: travesties, unreal compositions in which things look either too real to be credible or definitely unreal".[19]

While exciting, color's introduction had been so clunky that camera operators and cinematographers would often be so concerned simply with exposing the color film properly, that there wasn't a lot of room for exceptional innovative work outside of technical checkpoints. And then something quite interesting happened when paired with the Kodak single process negative.

It was not until Television, which was initially screening films in black and white, risked stealing moviegoers away from the theater, that filmmakers truly said to themselves that they needed to fully move to color in order to really have something that would maintain the theatrical audience during this transitory media time. Regardless, eventually when TV went to color anyways in the 1960s, the general consensus was that cinema would be left behind if they also did not make a significant push to incorporate color into their aesthetics as well.

2.4.2 Why Was This A Moment of Innovation

- **Initial Color Intensities Led to Emphasis on Color's Role in the Story**

Unexpectedly, the inability to really harness color's potential for a long while, and the refusal therefore to really see it as an artform led directors who used it to be forced to innovate its thematic relevancy and roles in the stories they were telling. It was bombastic at times and initially seen as an add-on. But while technology was

Historical Limitations Throughout Film Production's **33**

slow to catch up, and deals and relationships with the evolving medium of Television played a key role, that initial separation of color almost completely from Black and White in just about every capacity led to a new understanding of its opportunities in the medium. What it *could* do was wholly reconsidered, while technology took the time to catch up to other artistic achievements Black and White had already accomplished thus far.

- **We now have multiple visual languages to tell our stories**

Color can also be utilized as a time reference for story elements that before were not able to exist – only B/W existed in its varying degrees of contrast, which was wonderful but limited in scope. Introducing color not simply as reference for above notes on mood and character but also as symbolism and reference, was a game changer.

2.4.3 *Innovative Case Study:* **The Umbrellas of Cherbourg, 1964**

FIGURE 2.11 *The Umbrellas of Cherbourg* Still.

In Jacques Demy's 1964s *The Umbrella's of Cherbourg,* an entirely sung musical about young love interrupted by war to be perhaps/perhaps not rediscovered again, Catherine Deneuve and Nino Castelnuovo play the two leads, who are separated when he is sent off to fight in a war in Algeria.

The film was shot on Eastman Kodak Color Negative (Eastmanstock) ensuring the colors would pop off the screen, but only for a limited time. Negative prints were created for when these originals eventually faded away into an aged reddish hue, losing the edge of their color palettes that were chosen very deliberately to express mood, feelings, and the shifts and changes that happened throughout this piece – further supporting the entirely musical film.

34 Limitation Throughout History

FIGURE 2.12 *The Umbrellas of Cherbourg* Still.

The movie is bold from start to finish – from the very first time we hear Nino sing his opening lines at the mechanic's to the final scene of the film, this was not a piece that plays with subtlety. It also was a film that greatly benefitted off of the playful, almost otherworldly nature of the bold color schemes and wallpapers of its sets and costumes. These color patterns helped express the joy of the lovers' developing relationship in early pink and green hues, the sadness of the departure to Algeria in blue and green tones, and the expression of what ultimately was not to be in mimicked but slightly different color palettes later on. It is the epitome of the capabilities emerging of that time, of the ways that color was emerging – on its own and in tandem with film's technologies – to become a storytelling device in varying capacities for the moving image medium. This point is perhaps best articulated by Marjorie Baumgarten's "What Color is Your Parapluie?"

> On the other hand, the transition to colour became complete when filmmakers understood its creative potential beyond the realms of realism, and started treating it as a new artistic tool to empower their imagination. Colour brought to directors a number of artistic liberties to control audiences' emotions, and some of them stepped out of naturalism to engage with colour in a fantasy way, like Jacques Demy's *The Young Girls of Rochefort* or *The Umbrellas of Cherbourg*. A colour can mould a specific mood or carry out certain symbols and emotions; for instance, red is associated to passion, anger and danger. Natalie Kalmus explains that colours mixed with white suggests youth; with grey, it implies refinement and with black, dignity. All colours speak their own language, and it is up to the director to play with their connotations and sharpen the meaning of a film … Colour became a viable technology and contributed meaningfully to a film's style as directors stopped considering it as something superadded and used it to give an impulse to

the drama and implicate it within the narrative. They had more control over lighting, exposure, choice of set, costumes and props, but also over the colours of an exterior scene by deciding what weather, season of the year, or time of day to shoot in. As the technology improved, they also had more control over the camera's movement, choosing if an angle would include or exclude a particular colour in the setting, or minimize/emphasize a specific colour in the scene through long shot or close-ups. Colours also provide cues to read the face and body of actors, and forge connections between characters through costumes.[20]

FIGURE 2.13 *The Umbrellas of Cherbourg* Still.

In all of these examples, we have seen there were challenges presented to artists in varying capacities – some affective and beyond their control, some were sources of innovation that simply weren't quite working yet, but the process of investigation led to very interesting and unexpected discoveries. In each case, it's worth noting that they all have something in common – the filmmakers didn't give up. They kept going and expressing their ideas in creative ways while looking for the best ways they knew to tell their stories.

And so should you.

Notes

1 Michael Hiltzik, "Yes, Elia Kazaan named names, then made 'On the Waterfront' to justify his treachery," The Los Angeles Times, 16 January 2020, https://www.latimes.com/business/story/2020-01-16/elia-kazan-named-names
2 "Key Dates in the First World War," The National World War I Museum and Memorial, accessed 30 May 2022, https://www.theworldwar.org/learn/about-wwi/key-dates?gclid=Cj0KCQjwsdiTBhD5ARIsAIpW8CIwjQEmIU7aTTRWBRctGVdjKFCS5lCftWXtB-ovbLkJ_nygjhGs6YfwaAtlZEALw_wcB

3 "Nine Ways Artists Responded to the First World War," Tate, accessed 30 May 2022, https://www.tate.org.uk/whats-on/tate-britain/aftermath/nine-ways-artists-responded-first-world-war
4 "German Expressionism: A Break From Tradition," INVALUABLE, last modified 24 July 2019, https://www.invaluable.com/blog/german-expressionism/
5 Allyson Nadia Field, "Dorothy Arzner," Women Film Pioneers Project, accessed 18 May 2022, https://wfpp.columbia.edu/pioneer/ccp-dorothy-arzner/
6 Andreas Babiolakis, "Sound History in Film: Early Recording," Films Fatale, 27 May, 2020, https://www.filmsfatale.com/blog/2020/5/26/sound-history-in-film-early-recording
7 Sherri Rabinowitz, "Women of the Silent Film Era: Lillian Gish," Flapper Press, last modified 29 February 2020, https://www.flapperpress.com/post/women-of-the-silent-film-era-lillian-gish
8 Allyson Nadia Field, "Dorothy Arzner," Women Film Pioneers Project, accessed 18 May 2022, https://wfpp.columbia.edu/pioneer/ccp-dorothy-arzner/
9 Maria Lewis, "Dorothy Arzner, Mother of Invention," ACMI, 24 December 2020, https://www.acmi.net.au/stories-and-ideas/dorothy-arzner-mother-invention
10 "Great Depression History," HISTORY, accessed 29 May 2022, https://www.history.com/topics/great-depression/great-depression-history
11 Maria Lewis, "Early Hollywood and the Hays Code," ACMI, 14 January 2021, https://www.acmi.net.au/stories-and-ideas/early-hollywood-and-hays-code/
12 Ibid
13 Ibid
14 "History Matters," American Social History Project/Center for Media and Learning Center (Graduate CUNY) and the Roy Rosenzweig Center for History and New Media (George Mason University), last modified 22 March 2018, http://historymatters.gmu.edu/d/5099/
15 "Culture Shock: Theater, Film and Video," PBS, accessed 28 May 2022, https://www.pbs.org/wgbh/cultureshock/flashpoints/theater/hollywood.html#:~:text=In%201931%2C%20director%20Howard%20Hawks,known%20as%20the%20Hays%20Code
16 Trudy Ring, "New Film Showcases Orry-Kelly, Fashion Master - And Cary Grant's Boyfriend," Advocate, 3 August 2016, https://www.advocate.com/film/2016/8/03/new-film-showcases-orry-kelly-fashion-master-and-cary-grants-boyfriend
17 Ibid
18 Rachel Elfassy Bitoun, "A History of Colour: The Difficult Transition from Black and White to Cinematography," The Artifice, 21 April 2015, https://the-artifice.com/history-of-colour-film/
19 Ibid
20 Marjorie Baumgarten, "What Color Is Your Parapluie?" The Austin Chronicle, 19 July 1996, https://www.austinchronicle.com/screens/1996-07-19/532176/

3
FILM, DIGITAL, ACCESSIBILITY, AND CONTEMPORARY TRENDS

This section serves as a reminder that change is inevitable as technology evolves – and as we look at movement from photography to the moving image, we'll see that we are always striving to create images and experiences that put us into worlds and emotional moments that move us. But what we are also consistently coupling with that is *accessibility*. The larger conversation, as we will see here, involves who can access art, and that has **always** been a conversation. So as we talk history and mechanics of silver halide crystals to pixels, know that there are undertones that to this day need to be addressed and tackled, and without those battles it is arguable our work towards continuing to expand our storytelling capabilities wouldn't be as robust as it is today, and continues to be. These conversations serve as ways to not only understand and absorb the artform but also to ask informed questions about the democracy of its message – a key factor in the stories we strive to tell our audience. "Who," after all, do we make movies for? And how did our audience (and who it was we catered to) underscore how innovations in cinema occurred? Let's investigate.

Our first order of business is to understand where things all began – and that is with our grand predecessor – Photography. The response of silver to light was the impetus that began everything that we know about the image-making process and without it, we dare to say there would be at least a substantial gap before we saw any degree of the motion pictures we're able to experience.

3.1 Early Photography

As we know it, the recognizable photographic process began in the 19th century. But truly the concept began prior – *way* prior in fact. While a variety of philosophers, artists, and thinkers have used and explored the Camera Obscura in early

DOI: 10.4324/9781003286639-4

works, for our sake one of the first documented references of light refraction and imprinting was when Aristotle brought about the concept of the Camera Obscura in the 4th century, observing how the sun was able to be filtered through the small pinhole of a dark room to put an eclipse on the ground, so it could be seen without looking directly into the sun. The observation of the flipping of an image through the bending of the light rays, and the manipulation of the overall picture was one of our earliest experiences with controlling, duplicating, and transforming, in real time, the world around us.[1]

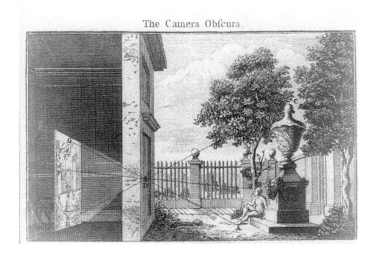

FIGURE 3.1 Camera Obscura.

Source: https://commons.wikimedia.org/wiki/File:Optics;_the_principle_of_the_camera_obscura._Engraving._Wellcome_V0025358.jpg, Attribution to Fæ.

Fast forward many years, and we find ourselves in 1826. A man by the name of Joseph Niépce actively works with a substance called pewter-coated bitumen in his quest to create a plate that will maintain the remnants of an image after exposure to the sun. After additional experiments with Silver Halide and Silver Chloride, there is some success but he cannot get the process to take less than 8 hours in the duration needed to maintain the image itself.[2]

Around this time, a painter named Louis Jacques Mandé Daguerre, who is very excited by Niépce's work, partners with him and works to further develop this exposure process by using silver-plated sheets of copper – subsequently fuming them with mercury vapor. As he continues working with Niépce, Daguerre is able to importantly reduce the exposure time extensively. This leads to an important landmark, which you may have heard of, that comes about in 1839. At a time when Daguerre had reached exposure times of just several seconds, the *daguerreotype* comes into the popular consciousness and is able to be utilized as a means of using photography commercially for portraits.[3] This has proven to be a critical juncture in the history of photography when it comes to the proliferation of cameras and the success of the medium.

FIGURE 3.2 Daguerrotype: Mrs. Logan and Mrs. Tucker, which Gen. John A. Logan carried in his pocket during the Civil War.

So to take a step back, what we have at this point is a format that has a reasonable literal exposure time, and a figurative exposure to mainstream culture, which is able to be utilized as a portrait-taking medium. This was a big deal as portraits were not necessarily common, could take a very long time and were previously primarily seen as a painter's medium. Critically, what we then will have several years later (1841) is a man named William Henry Fox Talbot arriving at the calotype process – where photographers can create a negative print. The negative print is a huge development – let's talk about why. A negative print, in which the brightest areas of an image are most responsive to light and subsequently most activate the silver salts during early development processes (silver halide crystals later on), allows a photographer to subsequently create *multiple* prints through reverse processing in the future of the same image. We now take this for granted, but at the time, what photographers were dealing with was a single-shot image, one and done. Talbot's creation of a negative print established both commercially and artistically a host of options that would open the door for our next key image moment.

In 1887 something quite interesting but also contentious happened with regards to film becoming more accessible … in rolls! Hannibal Goodwin, a Reverend from Newark, New Jersey, who was looking to take better quality images for his Bible studies, experiments with a formula for a substance called flexible nitrocellulose. This new formula and discovery enables Goodwin to expose images on of a full roll of film – the first of its kind. He files a patent for this invention a full two years before George Eastman comes out with his own line of photographic film in 1888, his made on paper – a slightly lesser quality both in durability as well as eventual image. But an entire roll! And two different kinds! This was big. Now, Eastman recognized that his product wasn't a favorite among photographers, and assigns one of his best assistants – a man by the name of Henry Reichenback, to design a base for the roll that's more durable but flexible, resistant to scratches, imperfections, and harm, and an overall better product. Reichenback comes up eventually with a formula that … hmmm is remarkably similar to Goodwin's. A patent is then filed for Kodak, and this new formula goes on sale in 1889, to wide appeal and success. Goodwin, of course, wasn't having it. He contested the patent, but unfortunately passed away while it was going through the court systems. His Goodwin company was then sold by his widow to a new company called Anco, who proceeded to sue Eastman Kodak, ultimately winning millions of dollars. Though the Goodwin patent expired not long after, he is not a hugely known figure for what is essentially a formula we *still* follow to this day.[4] In fact, the ONLY real difference between Goodwin's formula and ours? Acetate. Pretty remarkable, isn't it? Film IS really remarkable – so let's start talking more about it, now that we have …*a strong base!* See what I did there?

3.2 Early Film

Now that we have a *baseline* for where we are coming from with the early innovations of the photographic image and important chemical processes, let's turn our attention to film and its often overlapping timeline of breakthroughs.

Extraordinarily important for film are the concepts of Persistence of Vision and the Phi Phenomenon, so let's put those into our lexicons if we haven't already – and understand how limitations of the body are actually key elements for moving images to exist in the first place.

> The first of these causes the brain to retain images cast upon the retina of the eye for a fraction of a second beyond their disappearance from the field of sight, while the latter creates apparent movement between images when they succeed one another rapidly. Together these phenomena permit the succession of still frames on a film strip to represent continuous movement when projected at the proper speed (traditionally 16 frames per second for silent films and 24 frames per second for sound films).[5]

So if we pause for a moment – the very reason we are able to have the appearance of the illusion of movement in rapidly progressing images is because of an inability of our visual systems to process the stimuli fast enough. Hurray for all too human limitations! Film innovations often inadvertently followed at the behest of those involving photography, keeping in mind that artists and entertainment patrons were already certainly interested in both Photography and Theater – its two great parents.

Following right along the larger timeline of photography, as we saw with Daguerre's work in the later 1830s, we already had decently shortened exposure times. We also had the ability to reconstruct negatives thanks to Talbot's Calotype Process. So by the year 1877, when a bet arrives to find out whether or not all of a horse's hooves in fact do touch the ground, we find ourselves in a very unique situation. This is where Eadweard Muybridge's trip-wired 12-camera series of a race horse came into play, with his ability (thanks to his own innovations in shutter mechanics and photographic dynamics) now to not only record rapidly the images of a running racehorse in full gallop, but - importantly - to place these images back later onto a self-made Zoopraxiscope and find that when played next to one another, they in fact ... move!

FIGURE 3.3 Eadweard Muybridge, Johnston, F. B., photographer.

Source: digital id: https://www.loc.gov/item/00650866/

42 Limitation Throughout History

FIGURE 3.4 Eadweard Muybridge: The zoopraxiscope--Horse galloping.
Source: digital id: ppmsca 05947 //hdl.loc.gov/loc.pnp/ppmsca.05947

We also have Etienne-Jules Marey's discoveries in photographic movement in 1882, with his chronophotographic gun, a camera device that was actually designed to record the movement of birds. And so interestingly and worth noting, the first discoveries of the perception of movement in the rapid succession of the photographic imprints of these animals were in no way artistically inclined - on the contrary, one was essentially to solve a physics-related bet from an extraordinarily gifted photographer, and the other also was quite scientifically based.

So for those keeping track, at this point we have the principles of Muybridge and Marey, the Celluloid-based full strip by Hannibal Goodwin and Eastman Kodak, but hmm, what are we still needing? Ah! A camera you say? Yes! Up until that point we only had still frame photography cameras, and a key element that has not been discussed up until this point is the use of Sprockets, created by Thomas Edison who split celluloid and created the 35 mm roll as we know of it. This combination was precisely what was subsequently improved upon in the creation of the motion picture camera shortly thereafter.[6]

Such a device was created by French-born inventor Louis Le Prince in the late 1880s. He shot several short films in Leeds, England, in 1888, and the following year he began using the newly invented celluloid film. He was scheduled to show his work in

New York City in 1890, but he disappeared while traveling in France. The exhibition never occurred, and Le Prince's contribution to cinema remained little known for decades. Instead it was William Kennedy Laurie Dickson, working in the West Orange, New Jersey, laboratories of the Edison Company, who created what was widely regarded as the first motion-picture camera" - the Kinetograph, which would run at about 40 frames per second and exposure approximately 50 feet of film.[7]

What we have now is the capability of multiple images to be taken simultaneously, as well as a camera to take the photographs with. Hurray! But gosh, it still seems like something is missing, doesn't it? Ah yes. How do we *watch* what we've filmed? Edison once again calls on EKL Dickson who in 1877 created a device called the Kinetoscope, which could run the almost 50 feet of film in a kind of peep-show viewing format, between an incandescent lamp and a shutter for viewers. But! Edison never secured a patent for the Kinetoscope, so when it hit the public and was a pretty immediate sensation, the device quickly becomes copied and reproduced worldwide. However, like everything else in this book, we have to illuminate where it is ultimately limitation, and perhaps running into a pickle, that can lead to innovation and the creation of truly remarkable works.

FIGURE 3.5 Kinetoscope.

Source: https://commons.wikimedia.org/wiki/File:Kin%C3%A9toscope_et_phonographe_%C3%A0_cylindre_de_cire_coupl%C3%A9s.jpg, Attribution to Podzo di Borgo.

44 Limitation Throughout History

As stunning of discoveries and great as these sequences of creations are, they are always a series of one person's breadcrumbs coming on the heels of another person's. One brilliant mind leaves notes on photographic processing for another. Another brilliant mind doesn't leave a patent on a filmmaking device. And suddenly, movement continues forward because each leap - while epic, has some degree of limitation that necessitates constant change. It is inevitable and necessary.

And as exciting as the Kinetoscope was, it was big, it was bulky, and to some degree it was exclusive - these were sold for about $300 a piece which at that time was about $10,000 in current US Dollars. So these were not designed to be in everyone's home. Its screening partner, the Kinetograph, weighed over 1,000 lbs. The general public paid to come experience these, but they were not designed in any capacity for personal use, or frankly to encourage individual artistic directives yet.

> The Edison Company established its own Kinetograph studio (a single-room building called the "Black Maria," that rotated on tracks to follow the sun) in West Orange, New Jersey, to supply films for the Kinetoscopes that Raff and Gammon were installing in penny arcades, hotel lobbies, amusement parks, and other such semi public places. In April of that year the first Kinetoscope parlour was opened in a converted storefront in New York City. The parlour charged 25 cents for admission to a bank of five machines.[8]

Edison's greater fascination than recognition of the future here, ultimately led to the lack of copyright protection on these items - but that lack of protection was the world's gain. Because it was at an exhibition for Kinetoscopes in Paris that the Lumière brothers were inspired to arrive at their own crucial invention that changed where we were heading in both storytelling and accessibility - the Cinematographe.

FIGURE 3.6 The Lumiere Brothers.

FIGURE 3.7 Cinematographe.

Source: https://commons.wikimedia.org/wiki/File:Institut_Lumi%C3%A8re_-_Cinematograph.jpg, Attribution to Victor Grigas.

Crucially, this device could be both a camera as well as a projector and established the eventual (then) widely used speed of 16 frames per second. It was much lighter in weight, encouraging not only broader use but more dexterity of theme and story, and changed entirely the kinds of films that were being made. And very importantly - while not immediate - it also began to slowly alter the cultural take on moving image works to a kind of artform as opposed to a fascination of the mechanism, which was the manner in which many were lauded before in their commercial advertisement - *Come see this vitascope picture!* Now, the title of the film would eventually begin to be given more weight than the device on which it was created, allowing cinema to eventually head into a path all its own.

That movement would be further cemented by several key players, and two we will highlight are Georges Méliès and Edwin Porter, for very different reasons. As noted above, audiences to this point were still looking towards media that was familiar to them (and who wouldn't?) in their understanding of what exactly cinema was at this time - essentially moving picture shows. There wasn't tremendous length to the works, or storytelling. The Lumière Brothers and their Cinematographe had begun to change that perspective, with works such as *Workers Leaving the Lumière Factory* and *Arrival of a Train at Ciotat*. Both showed a presence that hadn't been seen before, as well as a realism and set of camera angles that were new and thoughtful. Time duration was being treated differently and something was in the air here. Change was underfoot, and technology's shift enabled that.

Enter Georges. With works such as *A Trip to the Moon*, what we have now is something unique that doesn't fully leave the language of theater, enabling viewers to maintain a grammar that is familiar to them - the proscenium stage, the static camera, and dramatic actors. Méliès's fascination with magic and his understanding of optics and camera tricks allows for these theatrical limitations to serve as an onramp for viewers to better understand this initial phase of what cinema has the capability to do. He came in at the right place, right time, and was just the person to begin the dialogue with viewers for how to tell linear stories in the moving photographic medium. However, the limitations in prolonged time were by modern standards jarring, and it would be Edwin Porter and works such as *The Great Train Robbery* - in which we would first become acquainted with the possibility of non-linear time and continuity editing. The film was a massive success and while it took a big gamble, was one of the first times that a filmmaker - as an artist - fully respected and understood their audience enough to take that leap of faith with them and understand the full scope of essentially what we had done in so many artforms before - experimenting!

These two makers made very different films but through each of their works, both the positives and the limitations, we are able to see forward movement once again - Méliès's embracing of the Theater, while limiting the full scope of his storytelling allowed viewers at that time the ability to find the artistic bridge forward with him, while still telling tales of non-realities. Porter's grittier tales of realism embraced some of the edits Méliès had established while including the epic parallel editing and continuity principles that we started to see furthered in larger works from that point forward.

As we have learned in this chapter though, for every step forward sometimes there is an interesting step ... minimally to the side.. And in the case of Edwin Porter, he'd eventually seen enough consolidating of power happening as he tried to continue making his work, eventually leaving the game following the exhibition and distribution dialogues that accompanied the industrialization of the medium. Theater owners and distributors weren't going to not make money, and artists as always were going to pay the price. On the one hand, this new era beckoned in the foundation of what we know today as the Theater and Distribution system for better or worse, and on the other the artistic integrity of artists like Porter was abandoned. The distribution models and theatrical contracts for films began to get put into place for copies and screening purposes, and simultaneously, it was around the turn of the century that the aesthetic of the narratives began to change.

The evolving storytelling model changed the nature of stories being told, which in turn made the Vaudevillian Nickelodeon a thing of the past, and the middle/upper-class aesthetic began to become commonplace on the big screen - in other words, those who would pay to see the films in the theaters that were now paying to screen them, would be catered to and recreated on screen. But the Vaudevillian Nickelodeons, which were able to successfully screen many of the Vitascope early picture shows to rapt audiences, were crucially - particularly in larger cities like New York and Chicago - able to allow for more diverse audiences as well as owners during incredibly segregated time periods. Per The Gotham Center for New York City History, theaters like Harlem's Gem Theater opened in 1925, and employed Black staff and projectionists at a time when many theaters were segregated and employing racist practices. These theaters also were screening work that featured actors of color, such as Charles Gilpin, whose work in films such as *Ten Nights in the Barroom* was so popular he was invited to join President Warren G. Harding at the White House for a special visit. Unfortunately, these structures could not sustain themselves as the moving image medium evolved, and especially with the arrival of the previously noted "Talkies" of chapter 2, technological movements caused disruptions before it opened doors for progress.[9]

So it's important to illuminate what is influencing artforms as they evolve - and how we end up watching what we do, as money, and often elitism moves the market.[10]

3.3 Early Video

In the development of video and digital imaging as we know it, there have been many developments that enabled this rapidly and expansively evolving form. This evolution has involved a multitude of discoveries and platforms, often finding one another - as we have seen - by an inadvertent discovery or happenstance overlap. Here, in order to understand the relationship between our previously discussed articulations in Photography, Film, and the manner in which these affected our push into the realm of digital and the everyday consumer's artistic voice, we will go over three of the primary important components of this era - but by no means are these the extent of the topics, discoveries, and equipment that would encapsulate the entire movement.

In 1965 as an intermediary bridge between celluloid and the digital era we are transitioning to, Eastman Kodak released an easier way to shoot film on a format called Super 8. Following a time when families and the amateur consumer were already filming on 16 mm, the company officially released a line of film canisters and cameras that were designed with the ease of use and processing in mind. Kodak further describes in their History of Super 8 -

Kodak introduced the Super 8 mm format, which included film, cameras and projectors. Cheaper and more convenient than previous formats, this is what really brought movie-making to the masses. Cartridge loading eliminated threading the film and was virtually foolproof. Made out of plastic, it meant no more jamming, which was a common issue with the 16mm Cine-Kodak magazine. And the entire 50-foot cartridge could be shot without interruption. The cartridge itself provided information to the camera about the speed (ASA) of the film as well as filter information for black-and-white products. Precision notches were set at specific points on the edge of the cartridge, activating mechanical or electronic switches in most Super 8 Cameras, most of which were built with battery-powered motors, eliminating the need to wind a spring-driven transport. In 1973, Super 8 film was made with a magnetic full coat strip on the side of the film that made it possible to record sound along with the image.[11]

FIGURE 3.8 Super 8 mm Spools.

As we have seen, however, often there were discoveries happening simultaneously in the field of the moving image that would impact the ways in which we moved forward. Super 8, while a big leap in consumer ease and capabilities, was still a format of film that required loading, specific cameras built for the dimensions of that particular cartridge, and eventual processing.

So as we approached the advancing century, we see a movement from film to the analogue tape systems of the VHS, or Video Hom System, to something that would change the game in a massive way. And that was Digital Video. Just four years on from our Super 8 systems, over at Bell Labs (part of the company Nokia), something very big was about to take place. That was the invention of the Charged Coupled Device, or CCD Chip.

Film, Digital, Accessibility & Contemporary Trends 49

FIGURE 3.9 Charged Coupled Device.

Source: https://commons.wikimedia.org/wiki/File:CCD_SONY_ICX493AQA_sensor_side.jpg, Andrzej w k 2.

The CCD Chip was created by George Smith and Willard Boyle, who would eventually go on to win the 2009 Nobel Prize for their work in the field. Like many times before, the initial research wasn't designed to be used to capture images in the way that the chip was eventually found able to do. The two were working in other areas focusing in computer memory initially, but their informative discoveries were incredibly key in the findings of light sensitivity as it pertained to image quality and retention.

With background from Robert Sheldon on the Charged Coupled Device,

The researcher's efforts were focused primarily on computer memory, and it wasn't until the 1970s that Michael F. Tompsett, also with Bell Labs, refined the CCD's design to better accommodate imaging. After that, the CCD continued to be improved by Tompsett and other researchers, leading to enhancements in light sensitivity and overall image quality. The CCD soon becoming the primary technology used for digital imagery.[12]

And additionally from the Nobel Prize Foundation,

50 Limitation Throughout History

In the sensor there is a grid of light sensitive cells that emit electrons when exposed to light, causing the cells to become electrically charged. When a voltage is applied to the cells, electrical signals are generated, which are used to build up a digital image. CCD was a breakthrough for digital camera technology.[13]

The Combination so far of the awareness of larger companies with the consumer desire to tell stories, and the new capabilities of the CCD (again, amongst many evolving trends) in capturing consistent and steady digital imaging, created an emerging synthesis that was about to open up new possibilities for many more makers than there was prior - even with Super 8. And what we're talking about right now is the introduction to the world of the Camera Recorder - aka, the Camcorder, which even though initially clunky and finding its way with large tape technology, gave a democratic access to the consumer as an artist and documentarian, that simply wasn't there prior. The intermediary period of cassette and magnetic tape-based consumer media was an incredibly important time period for American home-ownership of video-related work. Russ Fairley's discussion in Videomaker captures this inertia well.

The big change came when broadcast had a need to make their out-of-studio setups totally portable, and some major manufacturers created videocassette based systems for the broadcasting teams. Prior to this system, broadcasters had to use remote recording systems to capture the footage they shot.[14]

Important to also note, the Camcorder was created by an important figure and inventor named Jerome Levenson, who had actually invented over 500 different kinds of video recording devices during his lifetime. Levenson was an incredible contributor to the video industry's development and came up with some of its biggest innovations. Olivia Harlow follows much of Levelson's legacy.

He received his first patent in 1980, and just a couple of years later it was a reality—one that changed filmmaking forever. Of course, the camcorders we see today are very different from early models. When the devices first were made, there were no USB ports or handheld devices. Instead, motion picture was still recorded on cassette tapes, used primarily for television broadcasting. Soon enough though, the camcorder became a product for the masses, just like the Portapak. In 1982 JVC and Sony officially announced the creation of the "CAMera/recorder", or camcorder. Sony's Betamovie Beta camcorder used the slogan "Inside This Camera Is a VCR" and came to mainstream market in May 1983. Just a year later, Kodak introduced the 8 mm format. In 1985, Sony introduced the first chip-based camcorder "Video 8", and JVC introduced the VHS-C, a more compact alternative to the typical VHS cassette. In 1992, the first color LCD screen came to life, replacing the traditional viewfinder that necessitated squinting through a tiny hole to witness a scene. All in all, it wasn't long before easy-to-use, colored, high resolution video became the new norm.[15]

In about 1975, we had the introduction of the VHS and Betamax camcorders, which, while somewhat larger than we would experience later on, were easy to use and - crucial for accessibility remarks - the tapes could be recorded over again. The days of sending off your film to be processed once and never utilized again were done. VHS eventually did become the more popular of the two, though you can still find the Betamax in another iteration with the broadcast format Betacam.

FIGURE 3.10 VHS tape.

Important to distinguish here again, we are talking about video - TAPE. Cassette - TAPE. These materials were various sizes but all were a magnetic tape that was recorded on different polymer bases. The CCD and its digital technology hadn't yet fully merged with the consumer camera, and we are working with the re-usable but still very popular format of now public-accessible broadcast materials. That began to change in the 1990s, as it eventually caught up with the utilization of another element that other computer and television technology had been using for some time - the Digital Pixel.

The creation of the Camcorder, as well as the CCD Chip corresponded with another element that in truth, had been percolating in "iterations" we shall say, for some time. The two would coincide eventually, but let's examine that second element - the Picture Element, to be precise. Aka, the Pixel.

The Pixel, as know it today, according to Techopedi is "the smallest unit of a digital image or graphic that can be displayed and represented on a digital display device. A pixel is the basic logical unit in digital graphics. Pixels are combined to form a complete image, video, text, or any visible thing on a computer display."[16]

52 Limitation Throughout History

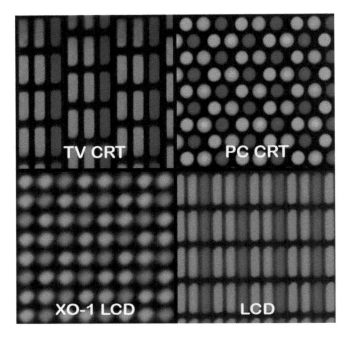

FIGURE 3.11 Different pixel composition comparisons.

Source: https://commons.wikimedia.org/wiki/File:Pixel_geometry_01_Pengo.jpg, Attribution to Peter Halasz.

To get to the point where we were able to have tiny digital elements that were made up of the primary additive colors Red, Green, and Blue exclusively, there of course was a bit of an evolution – and it involved the Television as well. Let's examine some of those key dates and moments that lead us to where we currently are with this crucial digital component.

As we've seen, we need to examine where we have come from quite often to see where we are going. And in 1861, James Clerk Maxwell's first accomplishment of the color photograph, with the overlay of RGB filters in photography lays the groundwork for the additive engagement of red, green, and blue that will enable us to know we will be able to utilize these sets to create essentially any color we will need.

A second big day for the Pixel is in 1926, when John Logie Baird gives a demonstration of his invention – the first "television" set, which sets the stage for the mechanics of the electrical system and line scanning that would be utilized in early mechanisms.

Baird's invention, a pictorial-transmission machine he called a "televisor," used mechanical rotating disks to scan moving images into electronic impulses. This information was then transmitted by cable to a screen where it showed up as a low-resolution pattern of light and dark. Baird's first television program showed the heads of two ventriloquist dummies, which he operated in front of the camera apparatus out of view of the audience.[17]

Shortly thereafter, in 1927 Philo T Farnsworth debuts his Cathode Ray Tube Television Set, which is able to use electron gun magnets to project images in lines on the front of a screen. Importantly, at this stage these sets are still using line images.

FIGURE 3.12 A Cathode Ray Television filmed in slow motion.

Source: https://commons.wikimedia.org/wiki/File:CRTslowmotion_PetesDragon.jpg, Attribution to Draconichiaro.

Then, in the 1950s – color TVs are introduced, with three electron guns now, one for each of our primary colors – red, green, and blue. Beams would hit an array of color phosphors called triads. These triads are still not pixels, and we are still dealing in lines. Not until the digital age do these get divided into the more current rectangles.

Then, in 1965 the Pixel, as we essentially now know it, was developed. With newer screens such as Plasma, OLED, and LCD displays taking the place of the Tube sets over time.

With the pixel in place, the questions about aspect ratios, storage, and aesthetics begin to explode and it continues to evolve and be a source of extraordinary innovation, causing a tremendous discussion about the nature of which method is preferable – digital or film. But what was the early dialogue like with that DV and VHS look, and how did it engage with the film aesthetic?

What we need to talk about here that is important is as video is developing, without any questions asked, it is automatically compared to film. And the first response to that is –

1 How is that even fair?

2 Why do we need to do that?

A huge question to consider is earnestly could we be further along in an entirely new direction from an innovation standpoint if we hadn't tried so hard simply to duplicate film? Let's discuss.

Digital did not have at its outset the Dynamic Range in terms of visual scope that film had - as Film had had some 100 years to innovate the manner in which an image was photographed. Digital Video also importantly has two ways of recording - Interlaced and Progressive scanning, the latter of which more closely resembles Film due to its ability to record at 24 frames per second (capturing similar motion blur) and to capture motion strobing. In interlaced scanning, two opposite fields of lines are rapidly interspersed repeatedly. In general, however, due to video's increased overall framerate of a general 29.97 or even 60 fps, its images tend to be comparatively *hyper* real, and have a completely different aesthetic - at least at its outset. But video also can be duplicated as many times as needed without any degradation, edited with ease on non-linear editing beds, and there are many, many positives that even in its incredibly early stages were present.[18]

So why did it get such a hard time?

Because it didn't look like film.

We had become so attached to what we thought by that point the upper echelons of this artform were supposed to be, that video was poo-pooed as lesser. And if we are being very honest - the fact that it was being put directly into the hands of consumers most likely played a strong role in that interpretation. Again, pulling the clouds back here and being very real about things - accessibility is huge in the perception of art's integrity. And when everyone is able to make something? It isn't exclusive any longer.

However, there were elements of early video that were incredibly nimble and a game changer in terms of quality of movement/form overall, due to the nature of the video cameras that were simultaneously developed and their lightweight physical structure. An example of early innovation that arose from the novel size and unique capabilities of camcorders in the early 90s, was the Dogme-95 movement. Dogme-95 was a collective of filmmakers from all around the world, who for approximately 10 years participated in a set of overarching rules, known as the "Vows of Chastity" that constituted guidelines for their films, in an attempt to return to form, and away from large budget Hollywood. The movement would produce 35 films in total before its filmmakers would part ways to pursue other kinds of projects. These rules are constituted below.

3.3.1 Dogme 95 Vows of Chastity[19]

i   Shooting must be done on location. Props and sets must not be brought in (if a particular prop is necessary for the story, a location must be chosen where this prop is to be found).

ii The sound must never be produced apart from the images or vice versa (music must not be used unless it occurs where the scene is being shot).

iii The camera **must be hand-held**. Any movement or immobility attainable in the hand is permitted.

iv The film must be in color. Special lighting is not acceptable (If there is too little light for exposure the scene must be cut or a single lamp be attached to the camera).

v   Optical work and filters are forbidden.

vi The film must not contain superficial action (murders, weapons, etc. must not occur).

vii Temporal and geographical alienation are forbidden (That is to say that the film takes place here and now).

viii Genre movies are not acceptable.

ix The film format must be Academy 35 mm.

x   The director must not be credited.

Video also had to fight for recognition in festivals as it wasn't viewed as *art* when it first began to be utilized as a visual storytelling medium. It simply was different in its aesthetic, and because of that, it wasn't being recognized - as was color film years and years prior - as a vital and important, competitive work. Many festivals wouldn't even consider *films* that were shot on video/digital cameras, and this perhaps delayed the development of the medium, but it's arguable that simultaneously it pushed its use and development into the independent film market, further developing many of the camera approaches that we see today. Dogme 95's *The Celebration* won the 1998 Cannes Jury Prize, helping pave the way for a more nuanced understanding of the capabilities of video. Its director, Thomas Vinterberg, often credits the artform with enabling many of the scenes to unfold and be created due to the flexibility enabled by this new camera size and scope.

As we've seen above, we've come a long way not only in the manner in which an image is absorbed from real life onto another medium, but also in the way that that medium influences viewer expectations, and at times levels of respect films receive. We have watched the evolution of the manner of storytelling evolve as the mechanism to tell the story changes - from heavier early kinetoscopes to the more nimble but directly related cinematographe. From a medium that was primarily shown in vaudeville nickelodeons to one that changed entire storylines to try to woo the upper middle class. Then a new artform full of pixels trying to make a name for itself within these same continuity principles created so long ago on a silver-halide-exposing base. Is it the right way to have done it? Who can say. But here we are just the same, in an ever-evolving system that continues to change and innovate. With luck, hopefully the door remains open for new makers to create strides in their manners of expression, so we can continue to find creative ways to tell stories.

3.4 Contemporary Trends: Streaming

3.4 is an overall heading, and an element like 3.4.1 size-wise is a subheading. I'm sure it is it's just difficult to tell here. Today, we hardly blink at a film being created on digital media, but the very notion of calling a film a *film* exposes the fact that this artform began as inherently a celluloid-based medium, and therein lies a conundrum. Is there a limitation any longer to using digital? And is the fact that we tried for so long to emulate what film was doing perhaps limiting us to the full scope of what digital pixels have the full capacity to do? Are we open to embracing the scope of what that is, and will we call it "art" when it finds us or be stubborn and possibly reluctant to embrace what the future holds?

3.4.1 Streaming Platforms and the Shift of Storytelling Timelines

This notion of emulation over innovation is very important when we discuss a massive player in not just the evolution of the film and television viewing industry, but arguably the production of the formats themselves.

While there are at time of writing a wide variety of streaming services, we will focus on Netflix and its history and evolution for our initial example.

We have to remember that before streaming, everyone would go out to the video rental store and choose what movie(s) they wanted to rent for that evening. The aisles were divided by categories - comedies, action, drama - and often there were staff picks chosen by the workers in the video store. Hmm, is this sounding familiar to our younger readers?

After the Internet began to find its sea legs in the mid-90s, Reed Hastings and Marc Randolph began the very early stages of a company called Netflix., Inc. in 1997. The company offered very early streaming options as well as video rental services as a number of drop-box locations across the United States. A few years later, in 1999, Netflix officially started offering an online subscription service where subscribers could order movies through the company website, and have them shipped monthly. Eight years later, in 2007, Netflix officially started offering its subscribers the option to stream movies online. Several years later it began offering streaming-only services in 2010, and by 2012, critically, had begun producing content for its platform with the launch of *Lilyhammer*, then *House of Cards* in 2013.[20]

The effect on the standalone video rental store began to be felt almost immediately. Locations like Family Video and Blockbuster, while certainly not ignorant of this incoming threat, arguably were not making moves to align with rapid changes in environments in a manner that felt timely enough for survival. While it may be easy to look back now and assume that these companies simply were passed by, if you take a look at the annual reports from Blockbuster, they were not only well-aware of Netflix's movements, but also were actively working with Enron at the time for possible movie streaming using fiber-optic networking. A move that ultimately didn't play out, along with optioning out of a deal to purchase Netflix way back for $50 million. But their downfall is much more complicated of course than simply saying they were left watching from the sidelines.[21]

FIGURE 3.13 Blockbuster Membership Card.

A key notion for us to continue thinking about in terms of accessibility and the impact of limitations is that video stores crucially made customers *go to them*. Not only that, but they also charged per item. A new platform that was accessible from home, and – again, this cannot be overstated as we are still seeing this with new films – was inclusive of a monthly subscription rather than a per-item cost, was a huge draw. And within about a decade, we saw a very serious and impactful decline of the former billion dollar in-house video rental industry – save of course for the lone Blockbuster storefront holding the line in Bend Oregon![22]

However taking a step back, the authors want to pose this very genuine question – we are still shooting very cinematically (and by that we mean upwards of the 4k spectrum) with full awareness that the streaming platform that is broadcasting these shows is in fact viewed on channels in which the quality is not in any way the same as as a Theatrical Experience – even on large, home television sets. One very pronounced example was the "Too Long Night" episode of HBO's final season of *Game of Thrones*, whose budget increased into the millions and multi-millions of dollars over its duration - not a bad thing, however, this particular episode became known for something rather fascinating from this accessibility standpoint we discussed above. That is that many viewers could not watch it as it was too dark on their viewing systems.

Now let's pause, dear reader, and break this down a moment in terms of the technicals. Above we discussed an important term that's called Dynamic Range. This term somewhat transcends mediums but in each case refers to the capability to handle extreme cases of difference - in visual technology the lightest of the lights, and the darkest of the darks. When you pair that with compression/decompression systems (or Codecs for short) that take large, rich files and make them broadcastable on streaming platforms - what can happen is a minor "crushing" of data information - and often, the loss of detail in darker areas. This can happen on many shows, in fact a recent episode of *Stranger Things* (one of Ingrid's personal faves) had somewhat crushed night sky nuances on a smaller digital screen. That show is in no way lacking the resources to be sure that doesn't happen in its original file, so absolutely, it's how it's being screened. But the point is, this is inevitable on certain platforms and this is key - this is how many people are watching this work right now. So a big question becomes, do you accommodate for that? Or simply accept the inevitable compression of your work, or - in the case of our *Game of Thrones* example, blame the viewers for the incident? In a somewhat remarkable rebuttal, cinematographer Fabian Wagner commented via Indiewire, "A lot of the problem is that a lot of people don't know how to tune their TVs properly ... A lot of people also, unfortunately, watch it on small iPads, which in no way can do justice to a show like that anyway."[23] There are also innate structural differences between even the best televisions and the theatrical screening space. And while televisions have evolved over time in tandem with the evolution of film - as we have seen them influence color's push in cinema - they are not by any means designed to screen 16×9, 6k beauties. So there is a distinct difference of formatting here, as there always was, and one that will perhaps always need to be addressed and reconciled in the ways that we prepare and create our media for consumption.

There were certainly artistic decisions for filming the extensive battle sequence this way in *Game of Thrones*, with a slow evolution towards eventual light bleeds, as the characters over time saw evil begin to dissipate during the episode. But our larger concern here is when you are faced with a very real limitation - that is, the knowledge that a very large percentage of your viewers do in fact watch shows on smaller devices now - you have a decision to make, and at time of writing we are not seeing many directors, cinematographers, and producers choose to move away from larger scale, deeply pixel-rich productions in favor of an understanding that there is a balancing act to be had with yes - calibrated televisions on some level - but on a larger scale the codec system that as of yet, has not caught up to the same degree as these 4k, 6k *all the k's* productions.

Now in addition to this, the unspoken elephant in the room is the theatrical model, and the financial difference in price between films and streaming platforms. You have statements from Steven Spielberg, from Martin Scorsese, from Christopher Nolan as the most published examples - that their films are meant for theaters. While we cannot speak for others, an implication from these statements feels very strongly to refer to the quality of format - of screen size. The writers are not taking a stance on elevating one over the other and want to be very clear that there is a very real home and place for the theatrical experience. At the same time, we want to be very clear that not everyone can afford at this point a $20 move, plus popcorn just for one person, when that is more than an entire month of Hulu. We're calling it like it is here. So what is the solution? Well, we've seen the evolution of the "Theatrical release, then streaming release," but this again points to our conundrum above if we are truly talking about a sincerity to technological soundness. A Theatrically shot film will lack quality when faced with its compression codec for streaming size, it's a simple fact - right now that is, who knows what the future holds. Do many viewers care? Not always, however as we've seen above with *Game of Thrones* - the answer certainly is not never and it subsequently can absolutely create an elite "gotcha" moment, whereby some viewers are welcome to take part in a key plot point, and some simply are not, based on thematic and technical decisions made without reference to viewing systems.

So how do we thoughtfully move forward as artists in this hullabaloo? By learning as much as we can about what we have, what we don't have, where our work may be seen, and how to make sure to bend in the breeze …

In other words, read on!

Notes

1 "History of Camera Obscuras," Camera Obscura Kirriemuir, accessed May 26, 2022, https://www.kirriemuircameraobscura.com/history-camera-obscuras#:~:text=The%20Greek%20philosopher%20Aristotle%20(384,leaves%20of%20a%20plane%20tree
2 "Niépce and the Invention of Photography," Maison Niécephore Niece, accessed May 25, 2022, https://photo-museum.org/niepce-invention-photography/
3 "The History of Photography," LUMAS, accessed 16 May 2022 https://www.lumas.com/history-photography/#origins-of-photography
4 Randy Alfred, "May 2, 1887: Celluloid-Film Patent Ignites Long Legal Battle," WIRED, 2 May 2011, https://www.wired.com/2011/05/0502celuloid-photographic-film/#:~:text=Hannibal%20Goodwin%20files%20a%20patent,classes%20and%20wanted%20to%20%5B%E2%80%A6%5D
5 David A. Cook, "History of Film," Britannica, last modified 16 February 2021, https://www.britannica.com/art/history-of-the-motion-picture
6 Ibid
7 Ibid
8 Ibid
9 Agata Frymus, "The First Cinemas in Black Harlem: A Look at the Silent Film Era, 1909-1926," The Gotham Center for New York History, 24 June 2021, https://www.gothamcenter.org/blog/the-first-cinemas-in-black-harlem-a-look-at-the-silent-film-era-1909-1926

10 Ibid
11 "The History of Super 8," Eastman Kodak Company, accessed 28 May, 2022, https://www.kodak.com/en/motion/page/super-8-history
12 Robert Sheldon, "What is a Charged Coupled Device?" TechTarget, last modified 1 November 2021, https://www.techtarget.com/searchstorage/definition/charge-coupled-device
13 "Willard S. Boyle - Facts," The Nobel Prize Foundation, accessed, 5 May 2022, https://www.nobelprize.org/prizes/physics/2009/boyle/facts/
14 Russ Fairly, "The Rapid Evolution of the Consumer Camcorder," Videomaker, 21 August 2014, https://www.videomaker.com/article/f22/17178-the-rapid-evolution-of-the-consumer-camcorder/
15 Olivia Harlow, "History of the Camcorder," Analog, accessed 25 May 2022, https://legacybox.com/blogs/analog/history-of-the-camcorder
16 "What Does Pixel Mean?" Techopedia, 31 August 2020, https://www.techopedia.com/definition/24012/pixel
17 "John Logie Baird Demonstrates TV," HISTORY, last modified 25 January 2021, https://www.history.com/this-day-in-history/baird-demonstrates-tv
18 "Digital Video," New World Encyclopedia, last modified 23 October 2017, https://www.newworldencyclopedia.org/entry/digital_video
19 Samuel Harries, "Dogme 95," Movements in Film, 14 November 2019, https://www.movementsinfilm.com/dogme-95
20 William L. Hosch, "Netflix," Brittannica, last modified, 8 June 2022, https://www.britannica.com/topic/Netflix-Inc
21 Marcus Tan, "The Downfall of Blockbuster," Medium, 8 March 2021, https://medium.com/an-idea/the-downfall-of-blockbuster-da69f6c8a536
22 Associated Press Staff, "World's Last Blockbuster Video Store More Popular Than Netflix," Chicago Tribune, 31 March 2021, https://www.chicagotribune.com/entertainment/what-to-watch/ct-ent-last-blockbuster-video-store-20210331-6nhms2go4ndldptojpmufexbk4-story.html
23 Zach Sharf, "'Game of Thrones' Cinematographer Defends Battle of Winterfell Against Complaints It's Too Hard To See," 30 April 2019, https://www.indiewire.com/2019/04/game-of-thrones-cinematographer-show-too-dark-battle-winterfell-1202129682/

4

FROM SOW'S EAR TO SILK PURSE

Creative Victories Through Limitation

Thus far we've observed an evolution during various transitional periods where changes took place that moved artists from A to B, all in the name of better storytelling, allowing them to find and refine ways of better cinematic expression, always moving, it would seem (just like a determined protagonist in a movie) around some kind of obstacle – or limitation – in the way. And as we saw time and again, these innovations greatly impacted filmmaking, often not just on a set in that immediate moment, but also down the long road to this very moment, from the introduction of synch sound recording leading to Dorothy Arzner's invention of the boom pole to the development of digital recording leading to movements such as the Dogma 95 canon and the proliferation of DIY filmmakers today.

But sometimes a limitation doesn't just create a new technology or advancement – sometimes what it does is help a filmmaker create a style that becomes their signature, an aesthetic that helps define who they are artistically. Because they lacked something they thought they needed, they had to invent other means of accomplishing what they wanted and in doing so, helped invent themselves.

And here, our dear reader, is where we truly start to pick up speed, where the rubber meets the road. Or in our case – where the film meets the image plane. Or, uh, light hits the sensor. Or … Well, you get the mixed metaphors.

Over the course of this chapter, we'll look at very different artists, all of whom used limitations to a distinct and deliberate advantage, the resulting works entering and remaining in their own cinematic canon, revered for their unique, innovative approaches – never possible without the deliberate, bold vision and willingness to step around the situations that challenged their visions. We will examine:

DOI: 10.4324/9781003286639-5

- The Development of Story, Character and Perspective through Pixar's *Toy Story*
- The Development of Artistic Voice through Maya Deren's *Meshes of the Afternoon*
- The Development of Rhythm and Timing with Frank Oz on *Sesame Street* and *The Muppet Show*.

4.1 "Just One Word – Plastics": Pete Docter on *Toy Story*

While we've seen that technological advancement is an important part of filmmaking, breaking down barriers and offering new avenues of storytelling possibilities, it can also have a boomerang effect. Witness the introduction of sound into the filmmaking process:

> Good news – we can now hear their voices as they speak!
> Bad news – the camera can no longer be as mobile because it is shrouded in layers of clumsy soundproofing. Meanwhile, the actors have to stand static around a microphone hidden in a vase of flowers or such.

Until a new technology is sufficiently developed and advanced, it usually offers only a limited peek into what is possible because of its embryonic – dare we say it (of course we do!) – limitations. It's happened over and over and over: sound, color, video … each have opened a new door, but only a crack until all the kinks and bugs were worked out and the technology reached its full potential. Even the advent of computer-generated imagery (CGI).

> Computer-generated imagery (CGI) is the use of computer graphics to create or contribute to images in art, printed media, video games, simulators, computer animation and VFX in films, television programs, shorts, commercials, and videos. The images may be dynamic or static, and may be two-dimensional (2D), although the term "CGI" is most commonly used to refer to the 3-D computer graphics used for creating characters, scenes and special effects in films and television, which is described as "CGI animation".[1]

You may be surprised to find out that CGI has been around longer than you think; it was actually already being used in the 1970s before it really popped into the zeitgeist with a film like 1982's *Tron*. Modern, slick, cool – it quickly began edging its way into more and more media as it became considered a significant part of the future of filmmaking. Even though it sucked.

Oh, are we being too harsh? You judge:

FIGURE 4.1 Still from 1992's The Lawnmower Man.

That's a CGI-created ... human face(?) from 1992. Yeah, that's the state of the art of CGI a year after James Cameron's *Terminator 2*'s release pushed the technology further than it had ever gone ... but only for recreating non-human characteristics. CGI could handle non-organic material nicely (albeit blocky and not very fluid), but people? Fuggedaboutit!

This was the dramatic limitation the creators at Pixar were (wait for it ...) facing when working on creating the very first feature-length film entirely produced by CGI animation, a little film called *Toy Story*. Pete Docter, writer, director (*Monsters Inc.*, *Up*, *Inside Out*, *Soul* ...) and Pixar employee #10, was there from its initial conception. In the gestation period of developing the feature's story, a point of reference the creative team used was a pre-*Toy Story* Pixar short film, "Tin Toy".

> *The sort of weakness of that film, I always felt, was the baby because it's horrifying – and it works for the story because, I think, from a toy's point of view, right? That the character that usually would be sweet or whatever is really kind of a little monster.*

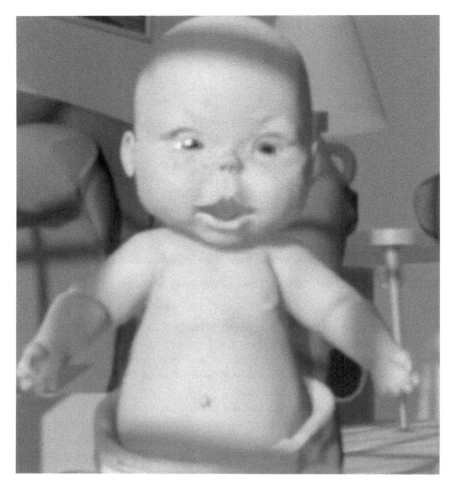

FIGURE 4.2 The Baby from Pixar's 1988 short "Tin Toy".

This is nowhere yet close to "uncanny valley" territory, that place where a computer-generated image looks very close to humans but not quite, causing our brains to generate suspicion, fear and even aggression. No, this is more like ... Mutant Baby – RUN!!!

And that's the best a high-end dedicated CGI animation company such as Pixar (backed by no less than Steve Jobs) could create in 1988 ... and this photo doesn't even display the awkwardness of its on-screen physical movements as it crawled and toddled across the room. So, when working on developing their first full-length film, Docter and fellow Pixar creatives knew it would not make sense to use human characters as the focus, as the technology – even in the early 90s – could not yet comfortably generate images an audience would enjoy. So, instead, they took the lessons from "Tin Toy" and doubled down on them.

> *When we look at Toy Story, we could barely do anything. Everything looked like plastic. So we're like, "Well, let's take advantage of that." We were like, "All right, let's take a page from Disney's traditionally animated film The Lady and the Tramp. If you look at that film, there are shots of humans, but most of the time it's like ...*
>
> *[Stands up so his head is out of the Zoom frame and moves around with only parts of his body showing. Sits back down].*
>
> *They did that for two reasons: one, it's really expensive to draw humans. It just takes double the time. And they're always tricky. I mean, Disney's animated Cinderella (1951) is an exercise in avoiding showing humans for that same reason. They told most of the story through the mice, to avoid having to draw people – and once again, that restriction probably resulted in a better movie.*

Choosing to lean into the limitation of CGI's technology's inability to create realistic humans, the Pixar team laid the core genetic DNA foundation for the entire film franchise by designing a story around toys who only come to life when a human is not in the room, thus achieving multiple bang for their buck. By removing humans as much as possible from the storyline, they would save time, hassle and expense, plus frustration of less than satisfying results. Then, when they did have to show them, they would either limit what was seen with the use of clever framing or use their unflattering CGI images to depict them as an antagonist force, such as the bratty boy next door who mutilates toys. On top of all that, these stylistic and practical choices had the deeply added benefit of truly connecting the audience to the toys and their plight; we are in their world, see things from their vantage point, from their perspective. We are fully empathetic with them, which make us yearn for them to succeed, a goal nearly every filmmaker strives to achieve.

So by not saying, "How we can make humans look better so we can create a movie featuring them," the Pixar team took insight from past movies and experiences and said, "Hey, this ugly human CGI technology isn't a bug – it's a feature." And now, over a generation and multiple sequels and shorts and spinoffs later, their initial limitation has shown the wisdom of that choice.

But wait – there's more! A quick anecdote about how a restriction such as the limits/expense of technology can actually create stronger – and in this case funnier – moments. Again, Pete Docter:

> *Anything organic is super expensive. Even now, it's more difficult. So we had this thing where, like just as an example, Syd, the bratty neighbor, was burning a hole in Woody's forehead by using a magnifying glass, and then he gets called away. Initially in the storyboards, Woody dunked his head in the dog's water bowl, which was kind of gross. And we thought it was funny. But then others were like, "No, no, no, water is way expensive to create. We can't do water." So we're like, How do we get around this?*

66 Limitation Throughout History

So, we took the camera, we lowered it so you couldn't see what was in the bowl. And then we made it a bowl of Fruit Loops cereal instead. So instead of water splashing out, you just have a few pieces of cereal – perklunk-klunk – and then, what that then added to, is when Woody brings his head up, he has two cereal loops stick to his eyes.

So it ended up being even better than water, you know? So all those kind of restrictions that make your brain go, "Oh, geez, OK, how do I get around this? What do I do exactly?" It feels like everything, at least that I can think of off the top of my head, everything that I've thought of as a negative at the time – when you look back at it, you're like, Oh, that was actually kind of a positive.

FIGURE 4.3 Woody enjoying a bowl of Fruit Loops, Toy Story.

Hey – somebody should write a book on that concept!

4.2 No Budget? No Problem: Maya Deren and Amateurism in the Quest for Artistic Authenticity

"I make my pictures for what Hollywood spends on lipstick."

Perhaps there is no other artist than the inimitable Maya Deren to turn to for inspiration -for not simply **that** a low-budget film can be done well, but in fact the film is done well **because** it is low budget. Deren, certainly the foremost experimental female filmmaker of her era and arguably one of the most formidable avant-garde artists of all time, argued fiercely and eloquently that in fact it was the very nature of the accessibility provided by these lower-cost sets, these "amateur" artists and their work, that allowed for the truest and most transparent of storylines to surface. In her tragically short but accomplished time as an artist, Deren achieved some incredibly varied successes related to filmic works – she was the first recipient of a Guggenheim Fellowship for filmmaking, and wrote what remains one of the most preeminent essays on film, "An Anagram of idea on Art, Form, and Film." She would eventually win the Cannes Film Festival's Grand Prix International, becoming the first female as well as American to do so.

FIGURE 4.4 Maya Deren in a still from *At Land*, 1944.

Author of some of the most famous experimental films ever made, including the masterpieces *Meshes of the Afternoon, At Land,* and *A Study in Choreography for the Camera,* Deren was also a very accomplished writer. One of her written works, the 1959 independent essay "Amateur vs Professional" expounds beautifully on her very specific angle that the individual and their thoughts, mind, and imagination, are the key ingredients of the success of the film. We include it in its entirety because it is that important:

> The major obstacle for amateur film-makers is their own sense of inferiority vis-à-vis professional productions. The very classification "amateur" has an apologetic ring. But that very word - from the Latin "amateur" - "lover" means one who does something for the love of the thing rather than for economic reasons or necessity. And this is the meaning from which the amateur film-maker should take his clue. Instead of envying the script and dialogue writers, the trained actors, the elaborate staff and sets, the enormous production budgets of the professional film, the amateur should make use of the one great advantage which all professionals envy him, namely, freedom - both artistic and physical.
> Artistic freedom means that the amateur film-maker is never forced to sacrifice visual drama and beauty to a stream of words, words, words, words, to the relentless activity and explanations of a plot, or to the amateur production expected to return profit on a huge investment by holding the attention of a massive and motley audience for 90 minutes.
> Like the amateur still-photographer, the amateur film-maker can devote himself to capturing the poetry and beauty of places and events and, since he is using a motion picture camera, he can explore the vast world of the beauty of movement. (One of the films winning Honorable Mention in the 1958 Creative Film Awards was ROUND AND SQUARE, a poetic, rhythmic treatment of the dancing lights of cars as they streamed down highways, under bridges, etc.) Instead of trying to invent a plot that moves, use the movement or wind, or water, children, people, elevators, balls, etc. as a poem might celebrate these. And use your freedom to experiment with visual ideas; your mistakes will not get you fired.
> Physical freedom includes time freedom - a freedom from budget imposed deadlines. But above all, the amateur film-maker, with his small, light-weight equipment, has an inconspicuousness (for candid shooting) and a physical mobility which is well the envy of most professionals, burdened as they are by their many-ton monsters, cables and crews. Don't forget that no tripod has yet been built which is as miraculously versatile in movement as the complex system of supports, joints, muscles and nerves which is the human body, which, with a bit of practice, makes possible the enormous variety of camera angles and visual action. You have all this, and a brain too, in one neat, compact, mobile package. Cameras do not make films; film-makers make films. Improve your films not by adding more equipment and personnel but by using what you have to its fullest capacity.
> The most important part of your equipment is yourself: your mobile body, your imaginative mind, and your freedom to use both. Make sure you do use them.[2]

FIGURE 4.5 Still from *A Study in Choreography for the Camera, 1945.*

This freedom of form on the part of the maker – this blurring of edges not simply in terms of crew, but also therefore of collaboration, allowed for a shift of story, of movement. Coming from a background in dance, Deren's incorporation of the body and physicality of space allowed an innovative approach to the way that her film stories manifested. Her match-on-action cuts that transformed entire landscapes hadn't been seen utilized in ways that transformed spatial planes and objects with such rapid fluidity, and to the extent she was using them to express emotion and visually convey storytelling. Her technical control over the 16 mm Bolex and deliberate manipulation of its 3-lens functions was a sight to behold. And for us, what was truly breathtaking, was that Deren wasn't looking to re-create anyone else's wheel by mimicking an already tried and true narrative film set – she wanted to experiment, she wanted to explore, and she wanted to create something new – and the way to do that was only through intentional limitation, in order to achieve creative breakthroughs.

As Ruth Grimberg eloquently elaborates in *Hundred Heroines*:

> Experimenting with camera movement, recording speeds and editing techniques to manipulate time, space and movement she sought to disrupt

the narrative and documentary conventions of commercial cinema. She did not aim to imitate reality but strove for a new reality to emerge that could not be created in any other art form. For her film was an illusionary, magical and imaginative time-form tied to a 'semi-psychological reality' though she always strenuously denied surrealism as an influence choosing to call her films 'choreographies for the camera' or 'cine-poems.'[3]

These Cine-poems often found their home at the distinct opposite end of the spectrum to much of the more narrative feature work that was being pushed and funded by larger Hollywood studios in that era. Because she would not be relegated to female-only spaces or roles either, she would oftentimes find herself head to head and butting heads with masochistic studio heads and directors of that day – it should be noted, regardless of genre.

Grimberg continues:

Deren never sought a specifically female space either in the art or political world and so found herself at times marginalized and exposed to hostility and derision in discourses still dominated by men. Most famously in 1953 at the Cinema 16 symposium her passionate proposition of a dual horizontal narrative axis and vertical poetic axis in film was humiliatingly dismissed by Dylan Thomas and Arthur Miller. Performing on-screen roles in her films, where she was also writer, producer director, camerawoman and editor, was both a solution to the financial hurdles of making a film and answered her insistence on the need of amateurism in securing artistic authenticity. Yet despite giving herself no screen credit for acting she was forced to defend accusations that her own mesmerizing performances, often cited as a precursor to the work of Cindy Sherman, were acts of self-promotion rather than a legitimate attempt to create a d-personalized exploration of identify. Her public arguments with Jonas Mekas, the 'grandfather' of avant-garde filmmaking who later wrote dismissively of the subjectivity of the female filmmaker, convey not only the strength of her structuralist convictions but illustrate the position she claimed as an artist not separated as a woman.[4]

Maya Deren's efforts to not simply make the films she wanted to make but also to experiment within a fixed set of variables that were inclusive of her own being as a tool in her filmmaking illustrate the necessity of exploring her work in our discussion of innovative creative minds. Her insistence on authorship and freedom, of the capabilities to play and explore the full capabilities of her favored 3-lens Bolex make her work in our example, *Meshes of the Afternoon* all the more noteworthy.

FIGURE 4.6 Still from *Meshes of the Afternoon*, 1943.

Meshes of the Afternoon is generally observed as Maya's masterpiece, but somewhat unbelievably was also her first film. Shot in 1943 for several hundred dollars, the film examines the journey of one woman as she returns to her home and confronts alternate versions (some would say realities) of herself, as well as an eerie being in a black gown and mirrored face. The film's varied interpretations (though Deren has often been noted to veer away from deep psychoanalysis of her work, opting to remain in the context of the film itself for true understanding of story), often revolve around iterations of identity, of societal intervention for women of that time period (compare the film's aesthetic to any of a similar larger budget during that time and you will have a very solid idea), or dream states and transformation of the self. Objects themselves within the film – specifically knives, flowers, the epic goggles – have been individually analyzed for meaning but as a whole Deren has steered away from clarifying.

However, as an experimental film, the piece strays from linear narrative, which is imperative for its overall success in the completion of the cyclical nature of the main character's confusing, often endless maze through her own home, trailing this otherworldly cloaked being and the strange continual appearance of additional versions of herself. Eventually, she is ultimately drowned in water that has somehow (Ingrid's personal favorite shot) been synthesized from one ocean frame to her own living room.

Deren's use of innovative camera tricks in tandem with editing that harkened back to the early days of magicians and theatrics at times, her beautiful match on actions to transcend landscapes, the extraordinary thematic implications of how multiple versions of the self can experience the same situation from varying angles but come away with completely different perspectives, and the nimble movement only possible from a free-legged camera, made this work one of the best we had and still have seen from one of the best Experimental Filmmakers in the field.

4.3 "They Have No Legs": Frank Oz on the *Muppets* and Beyond

Admit it – you weren't expecting this, were you? That we'd drag the Muppets into a discussion of cinematic limitations. You were probably expecting high falutin' art films and such, right? Well, those are here too, so don't worry. But let's not be too quick to dismiss popular culture ... especially something that has such an enduring, worldwide appeal. And if you're still being snobby about the fact that the Muppets' legacy initially comes from their work in the TV shows *Sesame Street* and *The Muppet Show*, they've also been known to make a film or two.

But what kind of limitations could exist with them? I mean, they're puppets – they can do anything, right? Well ... can they walk across the room in a long shot where we see their legs? Can they jump rope? Can they even just pick up a phone for criminy's sake? The answer is no ... at least not in a single shot. How do we know? Because someone who was there from the very beginning with Jim Henson told us: Frank Oz.

> *There's tremendous limitations with the Muppets and I can go on and on and on about them, but that's what makes it fun, too, you know? I mean, there's too many stories, but it's the limitations when you're filming the Muppets that really make it exciting.*

Mr. Oz went on to tell us that the sheer logistics of the working with the Muppets was an issue from their inception. As illustrated very thoroughly in his excellent documentary *Muppet Guys Talking*, the Muppets were brought to life by performers who wore their character on their arm above their head. As he explained…

> " ... *they have no legs. There is no master shot of the Muppets. It doesn't exist because there's no legs to have it. They've got to always be shot from waist up. And you've got to be careful in your framing because if you do a waist shot and you're too wide, then all of a sudden you got too much headroom in the frame. You've got to be careful in the framing there. And you also going to be careful down below because you don't want the performer's head to come up.*

Everything had to be staged and framed carefully to create the illusion that these iconic characters could move as if truly alive, and that meant working around the fact Muppets could never be filmed in a wide establishing shot, unless they were absolutely static, usually sitting and the character's legs had to be attached and adjusted into place; the audience could see the Muppets had legs, but the fimmakers could never show them using them. This forced the team to come up with creative ways to make the Muppets seem capable of dynamic movement without ever having the luxury of shooting a wide or master shot – an element many consider a fundamental aspect of filmmaking – to cover all of a scene's action. But Henson, Oz, and the troupe of creative puppeteers, directors, designers, and technicians all worked together to overcome this limitation and in doing so, created an approach that allowed the kinetic style and energy for which the Muppets became famous to flourish, helping to endear them to the world. (Brief aside: Oz repeatedly commented on how creative collaborating with everyone on the set was an essential part of the Jim Henson's leadership. He emphasized over and over that Henson would listen to an idea any crew member had and if he thought it effective, would thank them and then utilize it. Not enough can be said on just how important this kind of open and supportive environment is to overcoming any kind of limitation or restriction a production may run into.)

With characters nailed to the set (sometimes literally), the team had to make the shots interesting in order to invest life into the characters; often this lead to what became a hallmark feature of Muppet production: that of a character moving in foreground from waist up while the other characters remained static in the background. By tracking with the foreground character as they seemed to walk (or roller skate or bicycle or what-have-you) through the scene's environment while all the background characters remained stationary, the filmmakers created the illusion of Muppet mobility, even as they never showed any legs existing below the character's waist.

FIGURE 4.7 A penguin waiter "walks" by in foreground past a beachful of immovable characters in the background during a musical sketch from The Muppet Show.

74 Limitation Throughout History

This also gave opportunity for another signature element of the Muppets – as the foreground character "walked" through the scene, they would often cheekily turn to the camera to break the 4th wall to directly interact with us, the viewer.

Forced to work around such a severe restriction as immobile legless characters pushed the creators to create elaborately choreographed scenes to hide their stasis, adding a layer of *mise en scene* and technical accomplishment not expected of "just a puppet show", helping the Muppets establish a zestful aesthetic that continues to thrive to this present day.

But there was another specific limitation of the Muppets's basic design that helped create a different hallmark of Muppet productions. Again, Frank Oz:

> *If there's a prop like somebody picks up, Kermit, picks up a phone – he can't pick up a phone. Not possible. What you're going to do is you cut, switch angles, switch lens sizes, attach the phone, and then he starts talking with it. And then back.*

Not only would they have to move the camera and change lenses just for a character like Kermit to use a phone, they would have to swap in specially designed components that allowed it to look like they indeed could hold specific props … . and then back when the character was done with the prop.

FIGURE 4.8   Kermit with his good phone hand.

This constant need to shoot more shots and change elements of the character in order for them to do the simplest tasks could have been more than a tedious chore – it could have sapped a skit's rhythm. But instead, it became an opportunity in editing to better control the fast banter of the Muppets style of comedy.

> *The gestalt you talk about is created by the shots. In other words, instead of a master shot where Kermit walks in and picks up a phone and dials and puts it back down and has a drink of water and leaves, that's probably going to [actually become] six cuts of different shots. And that editing creates a rhythm – you help create a comedic rhythm that way. In the cutting we had more control in the comedic rhythm later on.*

Not only did this serve the Muppets well, helping create the rapid comedy they were known for, it also served Mr. Oz very well too as he moved on in his career; first as the creator of a little green creature who's featured in a series of films and TV shows that continue to this day …

> *Because Yoda has no legs either. So you really got to know technique. You got to know your shots and your angles and, and edit in your head how it's going to be at the end. You could do a wide shot. Sure. But just like the Muppets you've got to have a hole or rock or a table or something to show the legs. Then you can do a wide shot. That's why you got to prep each shot very well.*

Mr. Oz moved on from performing to becoming a director in his own right, first as co-director with Jim Henson on *Dark Crystal,* then sole director on other Muppet projects, and eventually to non-Muppet films, the first of which was his groundbreaking work directing the modern musical classic, *Little Shop of Horrors*, where he famously brought a one-ton animatronic plant to lip-synching life. Which was …

> *Impossible. Impossible. The physics wouldn't allow it. That's the limitation. And it had to do a fast patter song.*

But his work with the Muppets and the initial *Stars Wars* series prepared him to find unique solutions to this very unusual restriction.

> *I was rehearsing with a dummy plant earlier on in prep and we still didn't know how to make it go faster, and we were using video tape for rehearsals and recorded it at regular speed. And then we rewound it. And as it was rewinding, I said, "Holy shit, it's talking fast. It's going fast." And that's what opened it up for me. So we experimented with speed, we tried filming at different speeds, then at regular playback speed it would look like it was singing a song that Levi Stubbs had recorded for the film. But in order to do that, we also had to compromise and have Rick [Moranis] go slow. It was 16 frames per second when it was the plant and Rick, and that was how Rick could go slow enough so the plant could look like it was going fast.*

FIGURE 4.9 Rick Moranis with the full-scale Audrey II.

Having had so much previous experience dealing with the built-in limitations of the Muppets, Oz was able to tackle something that had never before been attempted, as he was able to trust in the process of working collaboratively with others to find solutions around restrictions that would not only yield the results he envisioned, but lead to something even better.

And as he moved on to no longer working with puppets but these very interesting organic entities known as "human actors," he carried that knowledge and process with him, making films with such legends as Steve Martin, Bill Murray, Michael Caine, Eddie Murphy, Nicole Kidman, Edward Norton, Bette Midler, Robert DeNiro and – legend of legends – Marlon Brando.

> *I do that also with regular acting. With Dirty Rotten Scoundrels, The Score, Death At a Funeral, and whatever else I direct ... because humans have limitations too, you know.*

Pretty good for having started it all working with "just puppets."

4.4 The Martini Shot

These are just a tiny few examples of filmmakers leaning into the issues they confronted and using them to take their work – and career – somewhere they might have otherwise never gone. There are so many more, from *Jaws* where Steven Speilberg faced a sinking mechanical rubber shark and had to resort to the new, better strategy of showing as little of the creature as possible in order to make it more menacing … Sam Raimi not being able to afford a SteadiCam rig so he nailed a camera to a plank of wood and had two people run through the woods with it in order to create his signature "Shaky Cam" shots in *Evil Dead* … Spike Lee, unable to afford the time, football players and extras for a pivotal scene in his sophomore film *School Daze* resorting to shooting the entire game via close-ups on the people's faces and cuts to the scoreboard … and on and on and on. If you want to see some ingenious – and often purposefully very funny – examples that are happening right this very moment, check out the account @shittyrigs on Instagram.com. It is exclusively devoted to documenting the wily, crafty and sometimes hilarious solutions filmmakers come up with in the heat of production. Just be careful though – it can become quite addictive.

Over and over and over filmmakers everywhere ran smack into roadblocks and restrictions … heck, Danish directors Lars von Trier and Thomas Vinterberg even created a "Vows of Chastity" with the Dogma 95 Manifesto to create specific restrictions of what filmmakers could not use in the making of their projects to force them to be inspired by the imposed restrictions. But whether you are following Dogma 95 or you only have a couple of dollars in your pocket or even if you have $100 million studio dollars, every film project brings its own unique collection of limitations, whether it's money, time, technology … whatever. Something is going to be limited in way you are going to feel utterly devastated by, and usually more than just one thing. But it's important you not view this as an impediment to your vision; as the filmmakers featured in this chapter have shown, reframing those problems and viewing them as creative and exciting opportunities, you just might discover the signature feature you will for all time come to be known by.

Notes

1 https://en.wikipedia.org/wiki/Computer-generated_imagery
2 Maya Deren, *Amateur vs Professional*, 1959.
3 Ruth Grimberg, "Maya Deren," Hundred Heroines, accessed 11 March 2022, https://hundredheroines.org/featex/maya-deren-2/
4 Ibid

PT. II
Practical Implementation

5

THE WHY OF WHY

Why Is Each Element of Production Important, and How Does Limitation Aid the Visual Storyteller?

The dreaded white wall … in the epic boring room … .

We try so hard as professors to push our students away from boring rooms in their films – but in discussions leading up to this book, the authors realized something important: Like anything else in life, there is a time and a place in storytelling for "the boring room." And in filmmaking, the boring room can *never* be boring – and that is the great challenge that at its core we all face essentially: When does our "boring room" override the other elements of storytelling that perhaps are so striking, that unfortunately we have to film it?

That is what this moment reflects on – the relationships of Pre-Production, Production, and Post-Production, and how each speaks to one another in the name of keeping the "boring room" exciting, even though that boring room in one instance (which we will discuss) has taken precedence over having a setting that is much more visually exciting.

What element of storytelling takes the cake when it comes time to put those pixels or silver halides down? Who takes home the trophy? Well, that depends who you ask, and (unfortunately) who has the money, sometimes. But GOOD storytelling, well that's another "story", so to speak … Let's talk about it.

Film is unique as a medium in its transition from words on the page to visual movement on-screen, and subsequent further cuts in a linear timeline. What you essentially have is a transition between several different modalities of storytelling, and by its nature then, a necessity to understand the final landing point of your words when you sit down to write them.

As we begin to make the movement towards film, many of us get comments back on screenplays (guilty!) of "cut this out" or "Too wordy" or "This won't be seen on-screen!" And that last phrase is extremely key for the writer: If you *can't see it*, you simply *can't say it*. Period. If you can master that, your writing will invariably

DOI: 10.4324/9781003286639-7

improve, because your brain will begin to reprocess the way in which stories are imagined in your head (seriously).

There is a muscle that needs to be active in the imagination as a screenwriter in which not only is your imagination free to allow for dramatic happenings to unfold, but it remains unencumbered by the brain element that yells "and cut!" As a writer you must remain open to your ideas, and let your characters live and breathe as real people, always - but also know where they will live and allow those restrictions to create opportunities for you to understand things like:

- Body Language vs Word Choice/Necessity
- Scene Relevancy to Overall Story and Arc
- Setting Visuals and Opportunities

A good friend of ours recommends that before any of her students take her production class, they take her editing class first. That may seem counterintuitive, but let's pause for a moment and examine the sound logic here:

Wouldn't it make a lot of sense to understand how a film is cut together in its varying shots, and unique grammar and language, prior to going out into the world and recreating those frames ? It's a fantastic approach, and creates for an early-stage filmmaker a very thoughtful understanding of the workflow needed to fully appreciate and understand the "Why" of a certain cadence and rhythm a scene should possess. Obviously rules are made to be broken on occasion, but understanding the reason that Match on Action shots exist in the first place and how they FEEL in the editing room when you cut them together yourself makes the on-set experience make a lot more sense as you frame them up yourself. You can see in your mind where and how they are going to speak to one another later. And that's a massive key to Production, which is perhaps one of the most challenging of our three elements in cinema, because not only are you synthesizing a formerly written artform, but you are simultaneously working creative muscles to storyboard and shot-listed where it is that these pieces of a puzzle will live, and the importance they have in succession to one another.

That seem like a lot of work? Yes, it is! And it should be, or to be honest you may be heading towards a very chaotic day on set without proper Pre-Production and organization. But when the elements are working, and the shots are coming together, there's no greater moment. Which brings us back to our boring wall! How is that a great moment, you ask, and why the heck would I ever choose that as a background?

As we produce films, we are constantly asking ourselves about the integrity of our projects. Let's expand on that for a moment: Certain elements of our production ensure something known as Production Value in our film, or, in other words, the overall quality of our film based on elements like costumes, set design, camera, sound quality, etc. If our script calls for a 9x6 cell block, and this is a realistic drama, then quite frankly we are filming in that space, it simply cannot be substituted. That is done for several reasons – to maintain the artistic integrity of the piece, as well as to add to the Production Value, as it is the appropriate Set Location. We cannot always choose extremely exciting visuals because quite frankly they may not be appropriate to our story. However! What we can certainly do is make those locations exciting through our Shot Lists, our integration of that Shot List with the Dialogue and how the two elements there – Pre and Pro – are speaking to one another, thus setting up our final element – Post Production – for success with a set of wonderful puzzle pieces and materials.

The editor in Post-Production is incredibly important and ever so slightly more independent (ideally) than our previous two components of production. Our Editor must maintain not only an understanding of a story but, importantly, a crucial ability to separate objectively when a shot simply is not serving that story. As we have mentioned before, film as it shifts and morphs to its final stage, is not unlike a caterpillar transforming to its butterfly debut – it can be that different in form from writing to final product (and we won't necessarily say which end is which sometimes)! But an Editor is a unique and talented individual who knows that there is a story embedded within the shots they receive – but someone who also knows (when given the freedom to do what they do best) sometimes those shots need to speak to one another in ways that may be unexpected.

One really fantastic example of unique editing moments found after Pre-Production and Production is in the *Silence of the Lambs'* (1991) Parallel editing Sequence, in which (I will try not to spoil too much here!) editor Craig McKay cross-cut a very tense sequence that director Jonathan Demme originally filmed linearly. It is through editing that the spatial distance between two sets of characters is manipulated in the eyes of the viewers, who initially believe two groups of people to be approaching one another - and that their timing expectations, based on years of film experiences and timelines, are really played with. Which, of course, is then totally turned on its head. This sequence ending, thanks to McKay, enables a tremendous amount of suspense to result at the final frame when we realize just how far away all the characters truly are from one another, and in this very frightening film, that help indeed is not coming for our main protagonist, Clarice Starling (Jodie Foster).

And it is the Editor who must ultimately turn our boring room, our possible obscure white wall, into something truly interesting and magical. But to pull all of our dots together, they cannot do this without some creative chutzpah from our Production Team, who in turn relied on the need for that particular setting as it was dictated as a necessity to story integrity and potential Production Value as well by our Writer.

And so dear reader, to ensure that you are a well-versed, multi-faceted maker who understands the creative muscles needed for each of these areas of production, please read on for exercises designed to improve your skills in them, hopefully in tandem and synchronicity with your fellow colloborators.

6
EXERCISES IN LIMITATION
Storytelling on the Page

6.1 Starter Yeast
6.1.1 A Spare Scene Screenwriting Exercise
Do you know what the hardest part of teaching screenwriting is?

If you immediately thrust your hand skyward and didn't wait to be called on before blurting out, "Getting students to write," you wouldn't be wholly wrong. That is a challenge, yes … but it actually isn't the hardest part. The hardest part?

Getting them to have something to write about.

And we're not even talking about big-ticket items like complex characters, big ideas and grand themes. No, we're talking about the basics: having anything to write about. At all! Meaning they don't have an idea for a script to write. Or, maybe more accurately, they don't have an idea they believe is worth writing; they have no confidence in their ideas, do not believe them to be worthy of writing. Possibly some are too nervous to share what they would really like to write about, afraid of revealing veiled truths about themselves (which by the way, are usually the best screenplays to write, if anyone is asking), but I would say the majority of new screenwriters just aren't really sure what to write about.

Our response is to give them something to utilize but – of course – loaded with restrictions: the "spare scene," sometimes referred to as an "open scene."

In acting classes teachers give actors a scene with very minimal, even banal, dialogue in order for them to learn how to create a character background and situation that would make such lines actually have a sense, meaning and emotional value. An example of such a scene could be something as simple as this:

DOI: 10.4324/9781003286639-8

Exercises in Limitation: Storytelling on the Page 85

           1
That's it?

           2
That's it.

           1
Oh.

           2
Oh?

           1
Yeah.

           2
What?

           1
Nothing.

           2
Right.

The scene is extremely "spare" – by themselves the lines have no real meaning; we the reader have no idea what is supposed to be happening in the scene. Yet, this very sparseness is what is the beauty of the exercise. For actors, it challenges them to create unique and specific meaning to mundane words and learn that even the most trivial lines can have a vivid and dramatic impact if the right situations are created.

And if it works for actors, imagine what it could do for writers.

The Irish writer Samuel Beckett used this same spare style to great effect in his famous existential play, *Waiting for Godot*, a play the British Royal National Theatre voted the "most significant English language play of the 20th century." And Shakespeare actually has very few specific lines of action in his plays – they are almost 90% purely dialogue … albeit, obviously much better constructed than the provided above example.

Well, if it's good enough for Shakespeare, Beckett and actors, then it's good enough for screenwriters.

Essentially what this exercise seeks to do is the same thing it does for actors – force writers to fill in the gaps that exist between nonsensical words on the page and an interesting scene that will be on-screen. And this is where the starter yeast metaphor comes in – the words give the writer what they need to get past the void that exists between them and having nothing to write; they have the "yeast" to start with that allows their imagination to add the "flour and salt" that turns seemingly meaningless words into something nutritional: bread! Uh, a story.

But the real key ingredient when doing this exercise is "heat"; bread won't bake without it and most writers won't write without it, "it" being some kind of time element such as a deadline, so, we give them an immediate one, such as before the class session is over. They have until then to use the given words of the spare scene to create a middle, beginning and end to a complete short film – no "To Be Continued" allowed.

Aside from the mere restriction of time and a deadline, another important one is this: all the dialogue of the spare scene must be used exactly as it is presented to them. No words can be changed, nothing can be added or cut from them and the order of the lines has to remain untouched. And boy, do they resent that! They so much want to tweak a line or add new dialogue in-between two lines – but they can't; they're not allowed to. They have to work with that limitation.

Now, that's not to say they can't add lines before or after the given dialogue section. Or write action in-between the given lines to set up the context of the lines being said – that's where they get to create the stories that give the spare scene's dialogue meaning. But the given lines themselves are sacrosanct and cannot be altered; once you use the first given dialogue line, you can not insert any new dialogue into the script until all the provided dialogue is spoken.

And you know what is so frustrating about this exercise? (For us, not the writers.) Every single time we have done it, it has produced some of the most creative work the students have done to date. Seriously. They come up with some of the best, most concise writing they have yet done. And we believe it is because the Problem With Choices has been negated due to the writer being given some "starter yeast" and then restricted in their use of it – the narrowing of focus takes away all the overwhelm of an empty page/screen and lights up a path of possibilities.

And once a new screenwriter has had the successful experience of creating a complete short screenplay within a series of writing and time limitations, their confidence in telling a film story increases and inspires them to tackle a truly original one.

6.1.1.1 The Deets

A series of spare scenes we created can be found in the Addendum section of the book, and you are invited to use them for your own "starter yeast" screenwriting exercises.

Filmmakers will be given/pick a spare scene to use in order to write a complete short screenplay with beginning, middle, and end within the given time allotment using the following rules:

- All the given dialogue in the spare scene must be used.
  - You cannot change any of the dialogue – it must be used exactly as is.
  - You cannot modify it, you cannot add to it, you cannot delete any of it.
  - Once the given sequence of dialogue is started, it must be completed.
- You can do the following:
  - Add dialogue and action before the given sequence.
  - Add dialogue and action after the given sequence.
- You may also
  - Write action in-between the given lines of dialogue – but no new dialogue can be written until the given sequence is completed!

Exercises in Limitation: Storytelling on the Page **87**

- The given sequence of dialogue can come at any time in the screenplay: beginning, middle, end – wherever you want it.

- Your screenplay must have a beginning, middle and clear ending. No "To Be Continued" or the like is allowed. It can be a surprise or twist ending or unresolved ending (such as exactly how will the events in the story impact the characters in their future is not made clear) but the ending has to make sense and be complete in the context of the story. No leaving loose ends hanging just because you ran out of time.

Follow all of these and tell a story that gives the given sequence of spare dialogue an interesting and understandable context.

6.1.1.2 The Goals

- To "take away the overwhelm" of writing when facing a blank page/screen.
- To build a confidence that the writer can tell a story when possessing only the most rudimentary of beginnings.
- To learn that by setting specific parameters/goals and a time limit, you can write creatively.
- That limitations do not deter creativity but, instead, help you focus on the options that are left.

6.2 No Dialogue – The Active Screenplay

6.2.1 An Exercise in Onscreen Exposition and Non-verbal Communication

Over 70% of how we communicate with one another is non-verbal. When you couple that with a visual medium, it's a wonder we even need words at all! Can you tell a story without words? (Short answer: very much, yes! Check out the "Historical Limitations Throughout Film Production's Evolution" chapter).

The frame and its relationship to non-verbal communication cannot be understated. Not simply mis-en-scene for setting, but body language and emotional impact for plot movement and fluidity of emotional arc – what do we need at its core; this is the conversation that accompanies this particular exercise.

Filmmaking programs tend to mimic the history of filmmaking itself – starting new filmmakers off by having them first create silent films that do not incorporate any dialogue. In fact, in his interview for this book, Pixar's Pete Docter shared this:

> *At Cal Arts, where I went to school, everyone made their own short films every year. The first-year student films were purposely not allowed to have sound. Part of that was because, well, that's a whole other technical bunch of gunk that you got to learn. But more importantly, it forced us to rely on visuals to tell the story. And of course, students don't*

like that. "I want sound! I'm not going to be able to do this without sound effects, or music. Waaa!" But guess what? The films come out better with that restriction.

Not all that surprising really, since the very motto of screenwriting is "Show, Don't Tell." But talking is a defining feature of being a human being, so of course filmmakers want to use it in their work. But it really is true – a picture is worth a thousand words, and films and TV programs generally operate at 24 pictures per second so … that's a lot of words that don't need to be said!

So let's take away the words – let's take away dialogue, which noted screenwriting guru master Robert McKee has infamously labeled a "regrettable second choice." Which is another great way of saying, "Show, don't tell."

Because as we enter a scene it's not the words that hold our interest, but the characters – their intent, desire, want, need; the question of whether or not any of those will be achieved – this is what we stick around for. And so at its core, when we break those elements down, they don't always need to be told in words and very often when they are (if we're being truly honest with ourselves) are overly verbose.

Of course, everyone loves a great line of dialogue; film & TV history is replete with immortal words spoken by characters – everyone has their own lasting favorites. But here's the truth about the process of filmmaking: dialogue is the most malleable component there is in a film. It is not written in stone or concrete … it is written in the wet sand that sits on a beach awaiting the next wave to wash it away. It is the first, last and most "middlest" thing to be changed during the entire course of writing, shooting and posting a project. It is modified …

- During screenwriting rewrites,
- On set as the actors who have been cast wrap their mouths around the words and offer alternatives,
- In the editing phase when plot elements or essential info needs to be clarified and actors have to be brought back in to do Automated Dialogue Replacement (ADR),
- or simply just cut out altogether.

Personally, we cannot count the number of times we have been involved or seen a situation where well-constructed and meaningful dialogue was cut from a film in the editing room simply because it was not needed once the action and characters' faces were seen on the screen. Sometimes a look is really all that's needed and the dialogue is superfluous. Pete Docter said,

I don't know how many times I've looked at the first cut of something and it's so long and boring and rambling. And then, when you have the discipline of forcing yourself to cut it down, it gets better. I think what happens is that you realize, "If I can only keep what's truly important, which ideas will stay?

So, dialogue is always in constant flux in service of the bigger story and objective of the film. It is the chocolate sauce and cherry on top of the ice cream sundae – a beautiful and wonderful and tasty addition, but – without the foundation of the ice cream (don't freeze up on choosing which flavor!) – dialogue is only a topping.

That's why film programs first work on the "ice cream" and save the dialogue toppings for later. And that's what this exercise does.

And it might seem simple on the surface: "Okay, you want me to write a script that doesn't contain any dialogue. Got it. Easy-peasy."

Whoa – not so fast there pardner. You better wait before you cinch up that saddle. Because yeah, writing a screenplay without dialogue may not seem too taxing … but you haven't yet heard what we want you to express in that dialogue-less script. Just writing action to show someone going somewhere doing something is not that hard – they're needn't be anything spoken to convey that.

But can you convey this without dialogue:

the emotional pain someone feels about the end of a romantic relationship that was caused by the other person not being emotional available?

Or …

the excitement someone feels about their future because they have just gotten the job they have always wanted since they were a little kid?

Or …

the longing an addict has for a hit of their preferred substance because of a recent tragedy, even though they are pushing 100 days sober?

Or …

the terror someone is experiencing because they must let someone know they have betrayed them and by doing so will end one of the longest and most stable relationships they have ever had?

Or …

You get the idea. Some aspects of these examples could be easily conveyed just by visuals, but the backstory and/or complexity of the situation would usually be much more easily told with dialogue. Easier, but better? Not necessarily.

That's the purpose of this exercise – to get filmmakers to expand their visual storytelling skills and consider different ways to visually convey complex information and emotions without resorting to dialogue.

6.2.1.1 The Deets

The screenwriter will pick one of the following scenarios and write a short script (under 10 pages long) depicting the elements detailed without resorting to using dialogue and NOT using

- Voice-over
- TV/radio/announcements
- Text messages
- Written letters
- On-screen titles/captions

(Oh yes – we know all of your slick dialogue workarounds).

What the writer should concentrate on are the images and actions that will convey the required elements contained in the given prompts.

And while the use of specific camera directions are typically forbidden in "spec scripts" (scripts that are written for the sole purpose of being sold to a studio, production company, streaming service, etc. and not intended for the writer to make), the focus of this book is on filmmakers and so it is assumed that most of the screenplays written by its readers are intended to be a project they themselves will make. Therefore, if a specific camera frame or movement will help convey the intention of the scene's moment, then they are encouraged. And tell you what, as a gesture of good faith, we will even get you started with a detailed scenario to work with, that you can follow along and tweak in different ways moving forward.

6.2.1.1.1 Scenario

Someone has just been broken up with their partner and must move out of a shared residence and find a new place to live. The reason for the breakup is that their partner is not ready for a long-term commitment and wants to end it now. (Another person is not the reason.) However, the protagonist had already envisioned spending their life with their partner and is devastated.

What the writer needs to convey:

- The relationship has broken up
- The reason for the breakup
- The protagonist's feeling about the breakup
- The protagonist must pack up and leave the place they have been living with their partner

- The new place where the protagonist will be living
- A sense of how the protagonist will face the future

Good Luck!

6.3 Less *Is* More
6.3.1 The Screenplay as a Hemmingway Haiku Exercise

When William was a high school student, he encountered one of the most frustrating experiences of his early life. No, it wasn't all the ones you're thinking – puberty, painful self-image, shyness, fear of the opposite gender, trying to figure out se…

Uh … okay, let's just move on.

No, it was not any of the usual high school stuff – it was a simple writing class exercise. Or, more accurately, an editing of a writing exercise. William's English teacher (the wonderful Mr. Richard Eccles) provided a page or two of an early Earnest Hemmingway novel and instructed the students to do the following: remove as many words as possible and still have a functional sentence. And trying to do so … was …maddening!

If you haven't read Hemmingway, part of his literary acclaim was his seriously spare writing style – it is stripped down to the bare essentials with simple, short and direct sentences and very few modifiers. Hemmingway was not an " … ly" kind of writer – very few adverbs survived his typewriter keys.

So, as teenager already having an eye on writing as something to which one might aspire but whose own "literary" style leaned on the idea that the more and purpler the words there were, the better, having to edit Hemmingway was utter torture for William – instead of adding more words, he was forced to attempt to excise all excess … of which there was frustratingly (sorry, there's an " … ly" word) few. And that was the point – Hemmingway had already carved his writing to the bone.

Little did William know that as difficult as that assignment was, it was excellent training for becoming a screenwriter. Because here's the dirty truth about screenwriting in the film business: no one got into the movie biz to read. If they wanted to read, they would have gone into the publishing business instead. No, they got into the film biz to watch films, not read scripts. However …

No project can be made without having a script written first (no film or TV program intended for a commercial audience, at least). The script is the blueprint of the film; just like a building must have a blueprint in order to be built, a movie/TV show has to have a script. And that means those scripts have to be read. By people who got into a business to watch, not read.

So that is why it is so important for screenplays to be as lean and tight as possible – the writer needs to entice the reader to keep moving forward, to keep on turning the pages and progressing through the story because there are scores of thousands of other scripts the industry must read every year. And any script that is overwritten,

92 Practical Implementation

overwrought and over-the-top with literary aspirations ... well, it's just not going to get read. And the movie won't get made.

Your screenplay is not about being published and admired for your vocabulary and writing acumen – it's either going to get the production made and be eclipsed – hopefully – by the movie that it becomes, or it's going to live a forgotten life in a drawer somewhere until the pages crumble or the digital components suffer what sci-fi writer William Gibson colorfully coined as "bit rot." Sad but true – there is very rarely in-between.

So the screenplay needs to be tight ...haiku-tight.

Hopefully everyone recalls what a haiku is – a form of Japanese poetry consisting of 17 syllables laid out in a very strict pattern of three lines, each line compromising of ...

5 syllables on the first line
7 syllables on the second line
5 syllables on the third line

And that is it! Anything else is not a haiku. You want to write a haiku, this is what you write – precisely and exactly. Nothing else.

Same with a screenplay – you want to write a screenplay, get ready to Hemmingway it up and bid most of your adverbs – and modifiers and long complex sentences and so on and such – goodbye.

So, in order to help screenwriters learn this, we created this screenwriting exercise with certain restrictions – natch – in place in order to get beginning screenwriters to really focus on what is needed and what is not. They don't have to go as far as a completely stripped down spare scene (although we have been known to do that once in a while), but they do have to rid themselves of many devices – some might say crutches – they are accustomed to use in prose writing.

6.3.1.1 The Deets

We have created a series of spare scenes[1] that can be found in the Resources section of the book that you can use for your own "starter yeast" in undertaking this exercise; the writer can modify them, re-order them, delete them ... whatever they want. The use of the spare scene here is only to have something to quickly begin with, as the focus of the exercise is not so much the story the writer will create, but the writing style they will use to create it.

The screenwriter will be given/pick a spare scene to jumpstart a short screenplay and write it while observing these following rules:

- No adverbs can be used.

- No words of more than three syllables can be used.

- No paragraph can be longer than two lines long and each one must convey only one thing: a character introduction, an image, an action, an emotion, etc.
- No parentheticals can be used to describe the delivery of a line of dialogue.
- Only what is said and done on-screen can be written, e.g., how a character feels or is thinking cannot be used (unless they say it aloud in dialogue or via V.O.).

Follow all of these and tell a story that has a complete beginning, middle, and end that also gives context and meaning to the supplied dialogue of the spare scene. Hopefully, you will not be as maddened as much as young William once was in his high school English class ... but if you don't feel at least a twinge of pain from being restricted (that word again!), then you're probably overwriting.

Note

1 These can be found in the Addendum section of the book.

7
EXERCISES IN LIMITATION
Storytelling on Screen

7.1 One-Take Jolly Dolly

7.1.1 An Exercise in Framing, Action and Movement with No Edits

One of filmmaking's greatest – and most unique – strengths is editing. Once the early filmmakers discovered the ability to edit their shots – cutting closer or further away, to a different angle, to a different subject, to a different plotline altogether – the true power of cinema was unleashed. Here now was an artform that did not rely on the constants of time and place – storytelling was untethered and free to explore in ways that were previously unthinkable.

So, of course, we want to take that away from a filmmaking neophyte!

Why?

Because by doing so, not only can they learn just how important editing is, they can also learn not to depend on it as a crutch; too many filmmakers rely on the "dumptruck school of editing," meaning they will shoot multiple takes of multiple angles without first formulating an effective plan for staging and blocking scenes and then "dump" all the resulting footage into an editing room and rely on figuring out an approach through it all there. And while of course great editing can improve a scene, it should be done in concert with well-thought-out blocking and shooting, not simply be the entire plan. Maybe sometimes it's a fair approach to a small scene that may not have a big overall impact on a film, but when it becomes the default approach … well, that's rather lazy filmmaking. To truly create a specific impact, a filmmaker needs to plan ahead and make good use of such elements as moving the actors and camera through blocking.

So, in order to get filmmakers to start thinking past the dump truck approach, we have the "Jolly Dolly" exercise.

DOI: 10.4324/9781003286639-9

To execute this, filmmakers are provided with a simple "open or spare scene" – a scene that contains only sparse, oblique – or even downright banal – dialogue with no action or camera description that can be interpreted in whatever way the filmmaker desires. You can find several examples of these in the back of this book in the Pt. VI Addendum section. Part of the fun of spare scenes is the sheer blankness of the scene's content (or maybe another word would be … "limitation"?) requires the filmmaker's creativity to come up with an interesting use of the purposefully bland material. Once that is decided, the scene must be shot in one continuous take, no edits, with the camera mounted on a dolly (or it can also be done handheld or using stabilizing equipment) and both the actor and camera are moved in order to create several different "shots" within one.

For some terrific examples of produced "oners" – oner being a slang term for a non-edited shot that stages the camera and the actors in order to create a dynamic and captivating shot without the use of cutting – just go to YouTube and search "Spielberg oner". Spielberg is a master of these and uses them constantly. And we're not talking about an ostentatious "Hey, look at me Ma – I'm doing a long-take shot that goes on for 10 minutes or so!" kind of oner. Those are obvious scene-stealers designed to be impressive, such as the *Children of Men's* climactic 8-minute long shoot-out running through bombed out buildings or Martin Scorsese's *Goodfellas* long Steadicam shot through the bowels of the Copacabana club. No, we're talking about shots that don't necessarily draw attention to themselves as they creatively support a scene's purpose without the use of editing. Speilberg effectively does these as a matter of course, and you'll find compilations of them on YouTube. And while there, check out Frank Oz's personal favorite, Orson Welles' "shoebox scene" from *A Touch of Evil*:

> *It's like a dance where he did it in one long take in two or three rooms and instead of getting a close-up then cutting to another close-up, the actors came to the camera to make it close. It's exquisite. It's choreography. It's beautiful.*

While it might be possible to do the same thing without moving the camera, adding the element of a moving camera forces the filmmaker to think in multiple planes of possibilities and go beyond just relying on static frames, which is all too often the case with new filmmakers.

7.1.1.1 The Deets

- Filmmaker will utilize an "open or spare scene" and create a context (genre, goals, character motivations, etc.) for the scene to be played in. Sample scenes can be found in the Addendum section.
- Filmmaker will design **one continuous take** (no editing allowed) to shoot the scene in, with the camera **mounted on a dolly** (or handheld).

- During the scene, the filmmaker must frame up the following "shots" as the camera rolls (again – no use of editing):

1 **Wide Shot**
2 **Medium Shot**
3 **Close-up**
4 **"Reverse Angle"**

Meaning the filmmaker must create a shot that moves the camera and/or the actor(s) so that they are shooting in the 180° opposite direction of the other shots.

Moving both the actors and camera is encouraged, but not required as long as one element is in play.

Again, **no edits** are allowed, not even "invisible ones" that can be created by merging/melding two shots into one in post-production.

Students submit an exported video file and the editing project file so the integrity of the shot can be verified.

7.1.1.2 The Goals

- To force the filmmaker to consider composition and blocking that is dynamic rather than static.
- To acquaint filmmakers with moving the camera to help tell a story.
- To confirm the impact and value of different frame choices.

7.2 A Lens by Any Other Name

7.2.1 An Exercise in Reexamining the Totality of an Instrument and Its Uses in our Art

Movements in art are often defined and remembered not just by the context in which they arose (Surrealism and Dadaism after World War I come to mind) but more pointedly to the aesthetic in which the art finds its hold. But both context and aesthetics are key, as one often informs the means in which the other takes hold.

The instruments that we use to tell our stories and express ourselves are also indicative of our times, as well as our means – but we are not necessarily limited to the means in which the instruments were created.

Consider the visual differences of Realism and Pointillism in painting. Both create with a brush using a paint medium applied to a canvas, yet the two could not be more different from one another, each creating completely different meanings and impact. And thus we now arrive at our camera lens.

This optical device has evolved in many iterations since it began in photography and filmmaking, increasing in focal length and optical distance, its f-stops and t-stops being innovated for stories and dynamic ranges necessitated over time. But rather than add onto it, today we invite you to explore an approach that is simple in its nature but completely dextrous and additive to your storytelling – removing the lens (somewhat) and breaking its light rays, modify their arrival to the sensor, also known as Lens Whacking.

7.2.1.1 Lens Whacking

When properly mounted, a lens is designed to accurately focus the image passing through it on to the camera's sensor; the goal with lens whacking is to alter this perfect alignment in order to create an image that is still usable but has much different qualities. In essence, the filmmaker is forcing the camera to record an imperfect yet creative image.

7.2.1.2 The Deets

In this exercise, filmmakers will need a DSLR camera body from which the lens can be removed and a short focal-length lens of ideally less than 50 mm. These are easier to grasp and balance in your hands and also allow for more control as you hover the lens just beyond where it is normally seated.

- By pulling the lens closer to the sensor, you are allowing objects further from the sensor to stay in focus.
- By pulling the lens further away from the sensor, you are allowing objects closer to the sensor to stay in focus.
- Light Leaks, Lens Flares, and Incredible variations in your depth of field are all key elements to explore and play with not only in the movement of the lens, but also the way it engages with your body.
- Importantly, as the lens is not attached to the camera you don't necessarily need to worry about your F-Stop. BUT you should take a moment to focus on Shutter Speed as well as ISO:
  - DO make sure Shutter Speed is twice your Frame Rate
  - DO Set your Focus to Infinity
  - DO Try using a 50 mm or below Focal Length
  - DO Start with your Iris open and adjust as desired
  - DO hold the body of the camera in your palm, and stabilize the free lens between your thumb and pointer finger.

Essentially, you are manually creating a tilt-shift lens that you're able to have an extensive amount of control over, creating dreamy landscapes and ethereal moments with all kinds of subjects.

Pro-tip: In Premiere, utilize your blend modes and opacity changes to really experiment with the ways that these images and dance and play together. And to our points regarding editing and the meeting of frames, continue to question the relationship between images and how they speak to and touch on one another.

Key Questions upon the group engagement of this activity:

1 Were there certain subjects that you found you were able to capture in an especially impactful way with this technique?

2 What did you find to be challenging about this activity? How will you work towards practicing with alternative techniques or approaches in the future?

FIGURE 7.1 Image of former Lesley University student Ash O'Neill during Lens Whacking Exercise.

FIGURE 7.2 A more fully dismounted lens, illustrating the broken plane and blurred lines typical of free-lensing.

7.3 Oh What's in a Frame – Where Are the Edges?

7.3.1 An Exercise in Spatiality of Framing, Continuity of Cuts, and Maximizing Lensing

What is the Value of the Edge of the Frame? What is its impact? Often we are so incredibly fixated on the subject matter within the frame itself, and its existence within a mobile medium, that we forget the lessons learned from our predecessors in art and animation – the stationary singular cell, or frame.

And so here we break down the medium into components that are simple and limited, but in the process allow a great deal of expression to happen once the artists are able to think in a 3-dimensional way.

Why?

By creating an understanding of the capacity to maximize movement, angle, and size within a confined space, we create the ability to not only understand the importance and singular impact of the shot itself with all of its unique components (angle, size, lens, subject) but importantly its subsequent relationship to the next frame as well as the previous, because in this exercise, all the frames can be rearranged, making the task of the artist all the more challenging.

7.3.1.1 Where Are the Edges: 3 Frames | 3 Ways

In this exercise, filmmakers will create a sequence that takes place over three distinct frames (three pieces of paper) no matter how those pieces of paper are placed together - vertically or horizontally.

7.3.1.1.1 What to Do

- Each maker/student will have three pieces of 8x10 paper, and an option of paint, crayons, colored pencils, markers, any 2D art supply capable of allowing them to create images on the page.

- The goal here is to tell a story – no matter how abstract, across three different pages, via three images. Is it narrative? In other words, is a person walking across one frame to another? Or is it more abstract – is your color scheme changing over time and a mood taking over the viewer who happens to be looking at these images when they are placed together? Well, here's the trick …

- The pages should be able to be arranged any way – front, backwards, rearranged, vertical, horizontal, doesn't matter. In each case, a new story will unfold based on your decisions that you make in your three images. THAT is the hard part. Can you find a way to create a story that with the same three pictures will provoke meaning no matter the way the images are arranged? It's not easy!

Choose edges very carefully, being very thoughtful in the control you DO have. Keep the following in mind:

- Where does each moment of the frame end, so the next can begin? In other words, where does my visual story stop being told in this moment?

- What happens in *between* these frames? THIS is where a viewer's relationship with you cannot be controlled but is also a magical space for imagination.

To reiterate, and as illustrated in our images below: when these three images are rearranged in any order, a story should be told. Your story should have a beginning, middle, and end in multiple ways, though how literal or abstract that story is, is completely up to you.
Can you do it?

Key Questions upon the group engagement of this activity:

1 What responses did you get from others on what they thought your "story" was to them? Was this similar or different from what you had been envisioning when you created your work? Why do you think that was?
2 What did you find to be challenging about this activity, and how does that impact the way you see yourself constructing your storyboards in the future for your shotlists?

Exercises in Limitation: Storytelling on Screen **101**

FIGURE 7.3 Results of Lesley University Student "Where Are the Edges" Exercise.

102 Practical Implementation

FIGURE 7.4 Students paint their multi-frame works to eventually tell a 3-dimensional story at Lesley University.

Exercises in Limitation: Storytelling on Screen **103**

FIGURE 7.5 Sample paintings during "Where Are the Edges".

FIGURE 7.6 Students at Lesley University work independently, painting three frames during their exercise, eventually to discuss the multiple directionality of these works.

FIGURE 7.7 Splatter! The exercise is a great way to encourage hands on materiality in otherwise digital funcationalities.

8
EXERCISES IN LIMITATION
Storytelling in the Editing Room

8.1 5 Edits To Tell A Story
8.1.1 An Exercise in Finding the Most Value in Every Shot

As we have seen throughout this book, the relationship between pre-production, production, and post-production is intricate and nuanced. The decisions created during one stage are inevitably impacted by decisions made in the others.

So by the time a filmmaker gets to editing, there are usually not an extensive number of surprises (though not always). But we have observed – time and time again – too many new filmmakers reach the edit phase and are in nothing but a hurry. There always seems to be an urge to rush through the post-production process and not give it its full due even though it's been said over and over and over there are three films you make: the one you write, the one you shoot, and the one you edit. When we try to give as much time as possible to the first two phases, why would we want a filmmaker to rush the last one, the one where many feel you finally and truly "write" the film.

When post-production is hurried, one of two things often happens: a film is cut too short or too long. Either the filmmaker will edit too quickly from cut to cut and not allow moments to take a needed breath to fill the air with their full impact, or they don't take time to have screenings with impartial viewers and get enough feedback to let them know that, sadly, they are not a cinematic genius with their early edits and, thus, allow moments to linger on the screen too long, draining all the life out of them.

Either way is a loss of the full potential of the film, but the worst may be letting a film run too long. Filmmakers always think they need more than they actually do. Frank Oz's view of this is:

DOI: 10.4324/9781003286639-10

In terms of editing I must say, I cut in my head all the time, so when I'm in the edit room, I know what I have already. But there are surprises all the time, especially as I get to the end of the first cut ... I'll be stuck. And what will often happen is I think, "Oh, I need a shot over here. And also this and this shot." And I realize: Oh wait a second – if I take this shot out and I take this shot out, I don't need either shot. Just cut from this to this. And often that's what I find – I find you don't need those or any new shots.

And talk about restrictions, every movie I've done, they [used to sell directly] to the airlines and you had to take four or five minutes out of your cut, otherwise they couldn't sell it. And of course, after I did the original edit, I'd say, "It's great. I can't take four or five minutes out of that!" But I have to. And I take four or five minutes out ... and never notice them. And that made it better, or made those cuts better because I realized I didn't need them.

You don't need everything you think you need – however, there are things you need that you may not have. And the biggest thing you need is signposts, emotional signposts and story signposts along the way. If you missed one of those signposts, you're going to confuse the audience. So the most important thing is get those signposts that are railings, whatever you want to call them, for the emotional and storytelling elements. Once you have those, you don't need the other stuff as much.

And in our interview with Pete Docter, we had an exchange with him about people filmmakers hanging on to too much:

I don't know how many times I've looked at the first cut of something and it's so long and boring and rambling. And then, when you have the discipline of forcing yourself to cut it down, it gets better. I think what happens is that you realize, "If I can only keep what's truly important, which ideas will stay? I really love this idea, but with a gun to my head I realize it really doesn't have anything to do with the main thing I want the audience to track." So length restrictions force you to get rid of anything unessential.

William Pace
I had a former student who went on to make an independent film. He raised the money for it and everything and when it was all shot and cut, he sent me a link to it and said, "Could you look at it and give input?" And I said, "Sure, absolutely." But when I opened the link and saw that the film was 2 hours and 20 minutes. I'm like, "No!"

Pete Docter
Good!

William Pace
"No – you get it under 2 hours and then I'll look at it. You need to make some choices and get rid of the fat before I can even see what the real issues may be." And he goes, "I can't," and I said, "Well, I'm not looking at it."

Pete Docter
That's great.

William Pace
Well, guess what happened two months later? He came back and was, "Okay, it's an hour and 56 minutes now." And, I was like, "Okay, then I'll look at it." Somehow he found a way to cut 24 minutes out of something that, before, couldn't be touched.

Pete Docter
You gave him tough love. That's great. Showing your work to people as you go is important. I know that a lot of students or other people think, "No, no, it's not done. I'm going to finish it first and then I'll show you, and you'll see how glorious and genius it all is." And inevitably if you do that, you've invested all this time only to have people say, "What's going on? I don't understand this, it doesn't make any sense." So as painful as it is, forcing yourself to show other people along the way, it's a way to give yourself perspective, to see it as your audience will. We have it[here at Pixar] built into our system to show our work to each other at about 12 different times along the way. In outline form, and script, and then at eight to ten different screenings. We show it to each other which allows us to see it ourselves with fresh eyes.

But cutting a film too fast and tight can also rob a film of its power; a gesture as small as a flick of the eye or a twitch in the forehead can convey so very much. Those minute gestures are tremendously important when on the screen in a close-up. Sometimes it is actually possible for a shorter film to feel longer. Why? Because the right rhythm of a good edit enhances important moments and can make the audience better connect with the characters and material as opposed to an edit that may be shorter but doesn't let them care about those things.

So how do you get to the point where you are able to recognize those moments that are ultimately needed in the cut and those that aren't? Well, it takes practice, it takes patience; it's a nuanced rhythm that paces human emotions and dynamics, and rebuilds them in a 2-dimensional plane when they previously existed in a 3-dimensional plane.

So you know, no big deal, right?

The best way to get to the point of understanding the benefits of **holding a cut**, is to literally do exactly that. And too often, especially when we are under the gun on a job for someone else or are in a rush to complete our own project, we don't feel we have the freedom to simply absorb a frame, an angle, and its relationship at different times and durations to the alternative shots around it.

So when looking online at the footage of a short film we have provided at *e-resources,* we ask Filmmakers to consider the following when choosing a scenes for this exercise:

A   Take note of all the available footage in this particular example. You most likely don't need it all.

B   Are there particularly evocative moments? Ask yourself very pointedly, what is it about this frame, this shot with this character that is speaking to me?

C   Based on your answers, how do we embrace and linger in this moment? Not only how long do we stay in the moment, but when do we leave it and importantly – where are we going? (i.e., what is your next shot – and where does *that* shot begin?)

8.1.1.1 The Deets

- Filmmakers are provided access to footage of scenes we shot for a short film and have made available for download and can choose a scene to edit.
- Filmmakers will be permitted 5 edits only to complete this scene. That's five cuts you get to make – no more. If you can do it in less, congratulations.
- The number of shots utilized can be more than five, but only five edits can be made.

If filmmakers choose to use footage other than the provided material, any kind of scene is welcome for this exercise but we encourage one that has at least two characters and is slower in its overall pacing and energy, to enable filmmakers to finesse its emotional tone.

Again, **five edits** are allowed, so make sure that these are important, and for every edit there is a specific reason you can explain the reasoning to someone else.

Students are to submit an exported video file and the editing project file so the integrity of the shot can be verified.

8.1.1.2 The Goals

- To force the filmmaker to consider the real-life timing of a shot and the value of different elements of its points of contact.
- To acquaint filmmakers with the intersection of spatiality of movement in the construction of emotional tone. Where do shots come together, and why? Are you moving from a close to a wide? What is the reasoning behind this and can you explain the timing you are choosing? If the answer is no, perhaps it's not the right move to make.
- To confirm the impact and value of different cuts in the impact of story and tone in a scene.

8.2 Physical Editing: The Frame as Reversed Exquisite Corpse

8.2.1 An Exercise in Subjectivity, Topic Imposition, and Editing Bias in Storytelling

"Phi Phenomenon." This is the inherent trick our brain plays on us allowing us to believe we are seeing movement in what is really only rapidly alternating still photos. Without it – and the Persistence of Vision – there would be no movies; only us staring at rapidly progressing images and left wondering what the big deal is.

In applying meaning to two frames that directly follow one another, our brain is able to create story in the "in between," often faster than we realize associations are occurring. This ability to draw inferences and references from all that have come before in our lives is part of the magic of filmmaking – the element of the maker-viewer relationship in which there is no control over interpretation.

One of the signature exercises often used to begin exploring this is the Exquisite Corpse. Under usual circumstances, an Exquisite Corpse (of any sort – many of us have done these drawing on paper at parties) assumes that one person does not know what the previous artist has filmed or drawn, with each subsequent image and imagined framed modifying and re-modifying the work, essentially creating a self-defining structure that creates its own language of meaning. A meaning whose only intentional skeleton is a pre-imposed topic (if any) given prior to the beginning of the creating.

As filmmakers, the Corpse is an incredible tool to understanding the elements of editing and loss of control we all will eventually experience when our films leave our nest, and, at the end of the day, the limit our narrative, experimental or documentary storytelling devices have when these films are absorbed by so many unique viewing systems. Experimental filmmaker Gabby Sumney explained to us how she uses this device to expand her work:

> *I'm in an ongoing collaboration with fellow experimental artist, Hogan Seidel. We're doing a play on the Exquisite Corpse—a surrealist technique of contributing to artwork with only partial knowledge of what the previous artist(s) contributed. We both pass back the same strip of film, adding layer upon layer until we decide it's done, and then we scan it and edit it together. We started it to test a mode of experimental collaboration I wanted to try with my undergraduate students. I think part of what makes it special is the improvisation that's so key to this mode of collaborating. We can only respond to how the film strip currently looks with more work either adding to or subtracting from the strip in front of us. We don't tell each other what we've done or how we've achieved that look, nor do we ask for permission to alter various parts.*

So, to provide early makers more control over our perceptions of the singular cut while working towards mastering ways to tell our stories, perhaps there is more to the Corpse and its capabilities than initially meets the eye – more to glean from its teachings outside of the editing room before we delve directly into its vast array of toolsets.

8.2.1.1 Using the Frame as Skeleton in Our Reversed Exquisite Corpse

Here, we will be turning the famous corpse structure on its head to innovate and think a bit more critically about the fact that we are all aware of our own subjectivity, biases, and the incredible differences we each can have in the interpretation of one single topic – how can **one** person change a film so vastly? As an editor, it's so incredibly vital to be aware of that limitation, and to embrace who you are, and what your work imbues in a diverse environment.

So rather than a topic, what we seek here instead, is a *consistency* to level the playing field. And in our case, it will be a consistency of FRAME.

You will need a group for this activity, and your topics are your own, and you will learn that our personal interpretations of even the most literal of objects can become quite untethered without structure.

Here we play with structure and watch how it stitches together the various shapes, subjects, objects, and configurations you encounter, and what they mean when viewed next to one another eventually.

8.2.1.2 The Deets

- Choose ONE kind of Axis
- Choose ONE kind of Perspective
- One person films One Shot – make it count.

Key Questions to Consider when Filming, and subsequently when viewing:

1 How does timing play a role in the meaning you are gaining from certain shots? Do you wish you had more time or less with certain moments? Why or why not?

2 When you wish you could cut, or change another person's angle – what is it about the previous and subsequent shots that you can articulate as being involved in that feeling? Is there additional potential to this "trouble" shot as is, were it moved elsewhere, or is the shot itself the issue? If so, articulate those feelings.

3 How does it feel to relinquish the control of the editing room in favor of a set moment in time with a physical camera? Do you feel more excited over certain eventual shots you see onscreen? Or does it cause a bit of anxiety over the entire process' outcomes? Sit with these considerations and think about what they mean for you in the two stages of production most examined here – Pro and Post. We are in an intermediary bridge between the two, not often encountered – but important to feel comfortable with.

8.2.1.3 The Goals

- Understand the relationship of individual shots as they stand uniquely in a timeline of images before arriving in any capacity to the editing later on.
- Know the role that your body plays innately in the construction of a narrative, split seconds before any cut is ever delivered whatsoever.
- Truly get to know yourself as an editor by watching the manner in which shots you do not expect or have familiarity with engage with a topic, and that directly

engages with work you made. Feel the way that you accept or reject certain patterns on screen, and examine why that is. You are a unique artist and individual before you are an editor – but to mistake that these qualities leave you as an editor, and that somehow you are purely objective in your thematic choices? Well, that is a mistake indeed.

In this exercise we intentionally reverse the corpse's surprise element but create a skeletal structure that allows for play within a defined space, asking entirely different questions in the final viewing process with regards to how limited visual scope and space in its consistency enforces narrative on a range of topics in our minds. Without the capability of non-linear editing, we realize in its absence the potency and potential that it has, and also, ideally, when it may not have been necessary to cut at all!

8.3 More Than Meets The Eye

8.3.1 An Exercise in Working Around, Above and Through Problem Areas in Your Footage, and How to Plan for Common Editing Conundrums in Production

Editors and Gray Hairs. It's entirely possible the two are synonymous, we give so many of our absolute cinematic pickles to our editors to solve, oftentimes without fully realizing it when we do. Let's take a brief moment before delving into this particular exercise's overview to discuss some problems editors can face, and why they happen in the first place.

In and of itself film is a linear mechanism – even films that run from a non-linear storytelling perspective, they still move physically from one frame on to the next – whether actual film frames or digital refresh. We always *move forward* in this medium, even if we're *telling* a story backwards. And as such, there is innately a singular way to process the images and sound that is being delivered to the viewer.

So when the images and sound are being spliced and stitched together in their quilt-like fashion in post-production, there is a limit to how these elements can be put together in order to make sense – let's talk about what we mean by that.

Say for example you are trying to move from a medium close up of an actress eating her breakfast croissant to a wide angle of the same situation, except – whoops, in the wide she used another arm to lift the breakfast bite. Well, now we have a continuity error (more on this below) that has the potential to throw the viewers off, and our editor has to begin a round of Choice Comparison based on available footage for that scene. This is where the game of puzzle pieces really begins – and ideally, an audience member is none the wiser. In your editing experiences it's possible that you learned some tricks of the trade.

Let's examine here ways that an editor's brain begins to first recognize, "Houston, we have a problem" to "Houston, we're moving the space shuttle slightly away from home base momentarily but you won't know it!"

Editor's feel in their body even before they see in detail that an error in continuity has occurred – a **break in linear space, and/or time.** So if we cannot seamlessly cut a match on action due to a number of reasons – here it's the wrong limb, but maybe the sun is out in one shot and behind clouds in another ... it could be for many reasons – we have work to do. This is where we need to think of ways to trick our audience – not in a bad way, but, actually a very kind way, to keep them involved in our film so they don't get distracted from our excellent story.

In the situation of Continuity Error above, and editor may:

1 Cut to a wide angle where the action was completed correctly.
2 Cover the cut with sound if it enables distraction.
3 Leave it be if the performance carries the scene well enough to distract.
4 Cut to another actor's reaction while perhaps L-cutting our original actor's audio to distract until enough time has passed that we can return to our main and needed actor, who initially messed their action up.

8.3.1.1 So Where Do You Come In?

This exercise is two-fold and designed for when you are feeling really ready to get connected to how Production and Editing speak to one another. We want you to go out in the field and film the following shots, but (gasp!) deliberately film moments that will not edit perfectly together. These will eventually need to be edited in a way that cuts around certain moments, and enables you to get used to the fact that an editor is a *problem solver* as well as an artist – and sees workarounds without being precious to the absolutism of shot order as vital to the understanding of thematics in a story.

8.3.1.2 The Deets

- Filmmakers will shoot the following scenario, and edit it together in a way that flows from a Narrative Continuity Standpoint – you will absolutely hit moments that ask you to choose your own adventure, and we welcome that – in fact, we WANT that!

8.3.1.3 Scenario

Two Actors have a beverage in a clear glass. One is left handed, one is right handed **during the first half of your shoot.** Then you will film the **second half** of the scene **with each actor switching their dominant hand.**

In the exchange, the two talk about a racy happening ... the backstory is yours to fill! One gets angry, then exits the scene, opening the door with their dominant hand. The other takes one final sip of coffee, and shrugs.

8.3.1.4 Script

ACTOR 1: So what were you doing there last night?
ACTOR 2: I already told you, I went to pick up the inventory.
ACTOR 1: I don't believe you.
ACTOR 2: Well I don't know what to tell you anymore, that's what happened.
ACTOR 1: I'm not going to sit here, and drink this while you lie to my face.
ACTOR 2: So why don't you just leave?
ACTOR 1: Seems like a great idea to me.

After preparing your shotlist in whatever manner or order you feel appropriate,

Film this scene fully in:

- Wide
- Medium on each actor
- CU on each actor
- Inserts on each actor's hands
- Inserts where appropriate
- B-roll of surrounding layout and environment

HINT: This should be editable in its entirety if there is enough footage of the location, exterior, some close ups … perhaps a little bit of the radio playing …? It should take some work but absolutely doable!

8.3.1.5 The Goals

- To show that by having to deal with and cut around the limitations of mistakes and imperfections, you are forced to be creative in your approach and try things you never otherwise would have thought of.

- To understand the relationships between Production and the Editing room, and the ways that they speak to one another, but allow for change to also occur when needed and when great performances happen but "whoops" *what were they doing with their hand??*

- To acquaint filmmakers with the fact that even with a defined shotlist, there is so much room for 3-dimensionality and workaround in the Editing Space. You are a reasonable, independent mind who very much needs to maintain independence for integrity of the story structure.

Have at it!

But also – at the very real risk of undermining the entire point of this exercise – do keep the following in mind; it's from our cinematography interviewee, Oliver

Curtis, a person who has spent his entire professional career trying to avoid continuity issues:

> *You know how obsessed we are about weather continuity, like when we see our exteriors and we've got to wait for the cloud to pass, we got to wait for the sun to come out and we do our best and we want to try and make it all match. And of course, you walk away at the end of the day and you had sun, you had clouds, you had rain, da-da-da ... And then they cut it together and it goes out and the audience goes, "Yeah, what?" Nobody notices. You've got to see things from other people's horizons, not just your own. It's so easy to become obsessed with your own horizon when actually other people are looking at it from another perspective. They have their own horizon they're looking at. And getting away from that fixation is key to being a filmmaker.*

The point? Not that there aren't real continuity issues that can destroy a scene, because there really are, but don't obsess over every ... single ... one. Certain nitpicking amateur online film reviewers entire raison d'être seems solely to point out that, in one shot, the water glass was half-full and in the next shot it was three-quarters full. Great. Hooray for you. You win the "Singularly Obsessively Focused On Trivial Continuity Issues Award".

As an editor, these are not the things to get hung up on; instead work on making the scene as great and powerful as possible so the viewer is so engaged with it to the point that even if they do happen to notice varying levels of liquid volume in a glass (or how smoked a cigarette, cigar, joint is, or that the name-tag was off in one shot and but on in the other, and on and on and ...), they won't care.

However, as an editor, if you have to cut a scene where the protagonist wears a very colorful coat in half the shots of a scene and doesn't in the other half of the shots and the scene takes place in real time in one location only (not that something kinda exactly like that has ever happened to us, of course), well ... good luck!

PT. III

Conclusions

9
THE DAY YOU HAVE NO LIMITATIONS IS THE DAY YOU HAVE NO CHOICES

Throughout our time together during this book we have examined a variety of topics, approaches, and persons, and gleaned a foundation of understanding together of the notion that art – in our case as it relates to cinema (though not exclusively) – is a fluid and malleable form. It is influenced by many things because it is created by human beings who themselves are impacted by the world around them. As such, artists are tasked with the onus of not simply taking in their world but reflecting on it, synthesizing, and coming up with some way of understanding how life works that is greater than the sum of its parts. That may involve anything from experiencing massive world events, to simply creating a feature-length metaphor for an emotional response to a breakup. Both are entirely valid expressions. But both are dependent also on the artist being able to cope with various challenges coming their way, beginning with the *inspiration* itself. Because truly, what is inspiration but a thorn in your side? Sometimes a pleasant one, but at its core it is something that stops you in your tracks causing you not to be able to move beyond a thinking pattern. That initial inspiration is a hurdle to overcome, and we overcome it through our art. When we frame our process through that lens, it becomes possible to realize that what we are being asked to do constantly - maintain nimbleness of creative mind, financial understanding, and cinematic production relationships – doesn't seem so far-fetched after all.

That understanding of each element of film production is your crucial foundation. Some of us (Ingrid raising her hand, here!) are writers at our core. That is how our ideas initially find expression – on the page. In film, we usually begin with a screenplay in narrative works, but please understand that specific workflow is not always necessary or required. If you are a visual thinker, and framing enables you to begin your inspiration process, or it's images that are lighting fire for you (and why wouldn't that be true for many of us in this visual medium?) then begin with proof

DOI: 10.4324/9781003286639-12

120 Conclusions

of concepts, with storyboards, with more visual elements that enable you to express yourself and find a way to reach that first articulation of thought - knowing that what we will eventually need though is that base skeleton screenplay. Because as critical thinkers in this medium, you're leaving this book knowing that the relationship between Pre-Production, Production, and Post-Production is in itself fluid, but that there is still a linearity of movement to how we generally go into production, and how these elements will speak to one another. Knowing for example how your words on the page can be envisioned into a shot list is a very strong creative muscle to develop. And this in turn will directly influence your final edit. Does that mean you cannot begin your creative journey with strong desires to shoot a certain sequence you are dying to try? Absolutely not - but be sure that it appropriately fits into the story you are looking to tell, and isn't simply an exercise in lensing with no guts to hold those images together.

This shout-out to style and substance calls for a mention again of our opening white wall discussion, and the necessity for visual brilliance at times (sure!) and at others, thematically appropriate banality. Remember to always return to your story, and ask yourself to be humble about what *it* is asking from you:

- Is it high production value with full-scale spaceships and laser sequences? Well, game on! Let's start budgeting because it sounds like that's where our money is going on this one!

- Is this story one where our location truly would be better in a subdued environment that would NEVER be visually bombastic? Again, there are ways to film this thoughtfully in a well-crafted shotlist and edit, to ensure that a cut is *never* boring! So that white wall? Don't ever fear it - just be sure it is appropriate to story, and for heaven's sakes, shoot the hell out of it!

But, hold on a second here - let's also address a very large elephant who has been lurking about, whose name begins with a capital D. What about the dreaded Deadline, you say? Well let's first begin by acknowledging one very crucial thought generally attributed to Leonardo DaVinci - Art is never finished, it's only abandoned (many thanks, Leo). You have to reach a point where you allow the work to simply … *be*. It cannot continue to be worked on forever, so think of it instead as moments in time. Allow deadlines to be a limitation that works for you rather than against you, and create timelines for your success in this medium. What you complete in a certain span of time is what you complete, and plan/budget accordingly for that timeframe. Allow deadlines and schedules to help you plan your projects and inspire you in the completion of your work, as opposed to thinking of them as restrictions. Let them be guide-rails that keep the wheels on the road, and also to keep a proper and truthful perspective of the scope of your project and its complexities. This will enable you to have a fully transparent relationship with the story you are telling, and the ways that you are capable *in this moment* to tell it.

This moment.

When this book was being written, it was quite a moment - the height of the COVID-19 Pandemic to be precise, and Bill and Ingrid would be remiss not to remark on the truly remarkable ways that the film industry was able to work amidst the tremendously challenging restrictions and safety measures that were placed particularly in production. This meant many different approaches, some that had not been tried before, many that are still in place even as we finish this concluding chapter. Testing protocols remain, masks for majority of crew, save for actors, often remain in place, complete redesign of food prep and seating designations for lunch, and an overall rethinking of spatiality and workflow became a logical part of planning a production. These are now a new normal in our everyday lives as we adapt and continue making films.

Once it was deemed safe enough to create production workflows again, new jobs were created on set to have COVID Safety officers. It is hard to imagine COVID testing not being a part of productions moving forward, and while not ideal, shooting in multiple locations, using equipment that had been disinfected or left for a certain duration enabling virus strains to die, maintaining distancing (which at least initially had a direct influence on lensing choices to say the least) all had a huge impact on the ways that we moved from page to screen.

There is also something quite psychological that seems germane: the way that art itself and the innovations that enabled its travel became the manner in which so many of us, frankly, made it through much of the past two and a half years.

There are relationships that speak to the discussions pertaining to the streaming industry - it was a virtual lifeline for many, as we were literally not able to get to the movie theater. Ingrid, for example, would have special *X-Files* marathons and *Golden Girls* nights with friends, which were able to be queued up on special streaming add-ons that Netflix and Hulu developed during 2020 so that friends and families could watch shows in sync with one another, knowing that this was needed. These were platform gestures that, while outwardly small, meant a great deal to many people. And as we mentioned prior, the notion of accessibility became paramount - all thanks to developments made earlier via digital codecs and the evolution of streaming as an international mechanism. In this case to keep people safe, and if we're being real - to help keep us sane. Cinema took us to needed worlds miles and galaxies away from a very difficult space we were living in, and that many still experience.

Did this change the distribution model for films and further solidify the initial theatrical and subsequent streaming release design? Absolutely. Many people simply were afraid for a long time to go back to a movie theater and did not feel safe in an environment that had a lot of people in it. The timing of the pandemic, and the ability of many viewers to stream allowed communication in ways that maintained some degree of social viability during a time in which mental health was hanging in the balance. The way that media and art was able at this stage to be transported thanks to digital innovations is paramount - working all over the globe and miles apart from one another did not stop the creation, completion, or viewing of a story. Literial physcial limitations became fulcrums with which to pivot to new points of inspiration. It simply changed the ways that these three elements transpired and in its way, the resulting stories that unfolded.

The impact of streaming during the pandemic on the film industry and the distribution model will surely continue to evolve, and as we previously discussed, the question lingers in the air about whether or not there will be adaptations regarding format changes per platform, or for that matter (as is happening at time of writing) further disruptions to the notion of the well-supported auteur. Platforms such as Netflix have made bold statements that after supporting large-budget films for well-known directors for some time, they will no longer allow such vast creative freedom, leaving a large question mark not only to the kinds of films funded by these super-ships of online services but also what this means for our notion of the film and series format in general. Borys Kit recently notes in the *Hollywood Reporter* -

> One thing many agree on is that the era of expensive vanity projects at Netflix, whether animation or live action (like Martin Scorsese's $175 million *The Irishman*), is likely over. "This tendency to do anything to attract talent and giving them carte blanche is going away," says one person. As always, there will be exceptions—this is Hollywood, after all—but in essence, this new era seems to be marked by one idea: discipline.

In its way, we cannot help but compare this to the evolution that's happened over and over again in cinema's lifetime, when the manner in which films are viewed has a direct impact on the ways in which the films are produced. From the Nickelodeon and Vaudevillian era giving way with its picture shows to the Cinematographe's more nimble but longer form 16 frames-per-second in a larger Theater - to the detriment of both the actors on screen and the diversity of the venue owners. Then the rise of Video felt a pressure to bend itself into a mold in order to simply be seen in festivals alongside Celluloid works. We wonder still about the directions that could have been taken aesthetically with those magnetic tapes had they not tried so very hard to mimic the celluloid structure and simply explored their own natural visual cadence. And now, we are watching in real time the interesting collision of the rise of the ever denser Digital Pixel - all those K's we've been talking about in the ever-increasing aspect ratios and dynamic ranges of the accommodating camera sensors - to their smaller screened compression system-needing home viewing systems.

What will it all mean, and where will the artform go from here? It's a truly fascinating question and one in which we are hoping you will be an engaged and creative player! We have enjoyed this time together and wish you the best in your filmmaking endeavors. Keep creating, keep collaborating, and keep innovating as you move through and adapt to each challenge... and may you experience many limitations and restrictions that lead you to creating your own signature style and masterpieces.

Happy Filmmaking!

PT. IV
Interviews

10
INTERVIEWS WITH WORKING ARTISTS ON THE ROLE OF LIMITATIONS IN CREATING THEIR WORK

10.1 Interview Introduction

When we conceived this book, we knew we wanted to provide insight that was beyond just our own, that we wanted to bring in people from all different aspects and kinds of filmmaking to share with us their experiences in the industry and how they have creatively dealt with the issue of limitations and restrictions in their careers. We were lucky enough to connect with a group of amazing and accomplished artists who took the time to submit to our badgering … uh, we mean, interview requests.

Initially we thought that we'd merely strategically place portions of their responses here and there throughout the book in order to highlight the various points we wanted to make, to show you the reader that, "Hey, we're not just making this up – really accomplished people believe/say/do these things too!" But as we collected all the interviews, we realized we had a treasure trove larger than we expected and shouldn't hoard it but, instead, share it … all of it. So we decided to add this additional chapter to the book and provide you with each gracious person's interview.

It's important to note that these aren't the exact transcripts of the interviews, as those would have been quite long and potentially – due to the nature of our back-and-forth conversations – meandering. So what we've done is edited the interviews and threaded together responses so they read as an engaging narrative where the context is clear and easy to follow. But everything here is what they really said – each person has signed off on what you're about to read.

Some of the names of our interviewees you might immediately recognize and some you may experience for the first time – either way, each one has a vast

DOI: 10.4324/9781003286639-14

reservoir of knowledge, and experience they are willing to share with others simply because that is the kind of person they are: talented, and giving. We are wholly in debt to each for their patient and nurturing support.

And each one wants you to know this: you will forever run into all kinds of obstacles, restrictions, and limitations … and that is a good thing because each one will be an opportunity for you to unleash your true creativity.

William Pace
Ingrid Stobbe

SETH BARRISH

10.2 Interview Excerpts with Seth Barrish

Seth Barrish is an actor, director, writer, professional acting coach, and musician. He regularly appears in film and television and is the author of the book, "An Actor's Companion - Tools for the Working Actor". As a director he is best known for his award-winning work with playwright Martin Moran and comedian Mike Birbiglia, with whom he co-directed the independent film Sleepwalk With Me and several of Birbiglia's Netflix comedy specials. He is the Co-Artistic Director of The Barrow Group, an award-winning theater company based in New York City.

My medium-long story: I grew up in Northern California, went to college, mostly at UCLA, was a theater major, music minor. After school, my first gig was as a Music Director at UC Santa Cruz. Then I came to New York in 1981 and I've been here ever since. When I got to New York, I did some work with Circle Rep, an off-Broadway theater company; they had just started a theater lab. In 1986, I started The Barrow Group theater company with my friend/roommate at the time, Nate Harvey. I began directing theater, in 1987 and then I started to dabble in film and television acting and directing. My first TV directing project was a self-produced 30-minute demo/pilot of a mockumentary about a theater company. We made it on a shoestring budget, shopped it around, got bunch of nibbles, but no bites. In 2001, I began to work with some solo show artists (Martin Moran and Mike Birbiglia). I developed and directed five stage shows with Mike, co-directed the film *Sleepwalk With Me*, and then ended up directing a number of his specials on Netflix.

I don't really differentiate much between film acting from theater acting – it's just acting. Although, films do have a few unique technical requirements (physical continuity and the ability to speak at normal volume) – you don't have to speak loudly so an audience can hear you. One major difference between film and stage acting is that in theater you tend to perform continually for a couple of hours a night and in film, things are shot over the course of many days, often out of sequence, with a lot of waiting in-between scenes. That said, as long as you're clear about what's happened in the story before the scene you're shooting, it works out fine. As a director, by the time you're shooting, so much prep that's gone on that you know where you are in the story at all times.

My early film performances were God-awful. "I would watch dailies or the finished product and be horrified by my performance. I had no idea what I was doing. But working on independent films I'd get weeks and weeks of practice to figure stuff out – "Oh, this is the workflow." "Oh, this is what not to do." And then, over the course of many years, I began to figure some stuff out.

Film and TV acting and directing can be pretty stressful. In theater, you're up there every night and as time goes by, you have a lot of opportunities to relax. In film and television, you're best served by relaxing right away. That can be challenging. Over the course of time, you learn techniques that allow you to, with luck, get relaxed pronto, and on a good day, be relaxed while shooting.

I always compare acting to jazz. It's like a mixture of structure and freedom. There are some physical things that happen at the same place in the script every time – this is the part where I set the table; I'll start with the forks and then I'll go for the knives; then I'll go for the spoon, etc., Along with this structure is a lot of freedom – you're free to think whatever, to feel whatever – lines can come out however they want to, etc. The structure and the spontaneity to me actually feed off of each other. Sometimes you can be a lot freer because of the structure. In other words, because my attention is on setting the table, I'm distracted from thinking about my performance. I'm just thinking, "Forks … now knives … now spoons." It's kind of like a meditation – a mantra that allows you to be really free and still get surprised, even though you've done like 12 takes of something.

I mean, every once in a while you run into directors that have a very specific idea of what they want and they'll just say, "Say it like this and at this rhythm." or "Be more mean!" That sort of stuff. And, I think it's safe to say, for most actors, including myself … that's a total drag. But you know, there's a hierarchy. So it's not like I can say, "Well, I'm just going to do what I want and fuck that." I have to be respectful to the hierarchy. I think it's a much better situation for all parties when there's a sense of collaboration and openness and people are given space to do what they do best.

I just did a film directed by Ray Romano and it was one of my favorite director-actor experiences. I just had one scene with Laurie Metcalfe, and Ray was totally chill, going, "Yeah, OK. So, like, maybe go over to the sink and wash your hands, you know? And then you'll get a thing to dry, so do that and then put on the gloves for the examination. You'll do that and then and this is where you go. And then when you're done, on this line, you can kind of take the gloves off, maybe throw it away in the trash." That was so helpful. I didn't have to worry, like, " I got to come up with a bunch of stuff to do." I just went from task to task and found myself completely relaxed. I didn't have any time to think about my performance at all.

Here's an example of direction that kinda sucked ... I was on an episodic show, and they did camera blocking. I was loosening up, saying the lines, coming up with physical activities, etc. And I remember thinking, *Wow, I feel really loose. This is great.* And then the director came in and said, "Hah! That's so funny. Wouldn't it be funny if you actually did it *that* way? Now give me a *real* performance!"

And ... it was beyond the drag. My entire performance got all forced and self-conscious. As actors, this is one of the challenges we need to deal with both in stage and on film – directors who don't understand acting process. When this happens, we engage in a kind of dance where we have to figure out, *What can I do to give them what they want, but also stay true to what I think is best?* So you end up translating. Like the director says, "Performance," and I kind of hear that and go, *Well, I'll ignore that one.* I mean, I never say this to the director ... I don't go, "I'm going to ignore that." You know, I just kind of go like, "All right." Then I begin to translate what the director said to 'Seth-speak:' *It seems like he wants it to have more urgency or something. Hmmmm ... if I try to make things more urgent, it's gonna look forced. What can I do that might give them the result they're looking for? Maybe I'll just tell myself that I got another meeting to get to. Maybe playing with that time deadline in mind might create a sense of urgency for the audience?* Then I just play with that in mind and, with luck, it gives them what they want. That said, it's pretty hard to get to the point where your "director-proof." I'm not there yet and I don't know anyone who is."Director-proof " would mean that no matter what the director does and says, somehow you're just always brilliant. I mean, you could pick the most iconic actors. I don't care who it is: Brando, Meryl Streep, whatever generation ... Ryan Gosling, Juliette Binoche, anybody that you like. All of them have done things where you're looking at and think, "They weren't as good as they usually are." I think some of that may have to do with whatever happened on that set.

As for film directing, I find it challenging. It's anxiety-producing for me. I would describe myself, metaphorically, as a turtle. I really like working through things in a slow, easygoing manner. And so many times in film situations it's, "Make a decision now!" And all these people are waiting on me. And it's difficult to figure out how to relax within that.

I've never been in a work situation – theater or film – where they said, "Just do whatever you want, whenever you want." It's not like that. You're working within parameters – the space you're in; the size of the budget; the location; lighting limitations; all of that stuff. The way I look at it: *Necessity is the mother of invention.* It *is* what it *is*. "We're losing the light, we got to go!" or "We need to get 12 pages shot today so we're going to make what was two scenes one." or "We do not have time to shoot that scene – can we rewrite this thing so that that scene doesn't exist?"

There are so many things that show up like that. And part of the game, I think, is learning to go with the flow. It's our job to ride with it and get the job done.

When we did *Sleepwalk With Me*, after we did the whole shoot and edited the film, we knew that it wasn't working. But we had a ripcord plan. The movie was loosely based on a theater piece where Mike was breaking the fourth wall. So we knew that if the first pass didn't work, we could do a bunch of reshoots of Mike talking to camera and that would move from story point to story point in sort of alternative way that would allow us to jump time and space – not just move through time chronologically. We were on a very limited budget, but somehow we got like nine days of reshooting. We got in a car and hit the road. Mike drove and talked to the camera, the DP in the passenger seat. The sound guy and I were in the back seat with cans [headphones] on. It was an incredibly crazy thing and everything was shot in real time. Mike would drive and pay a toll or whatever and turn and talk to the camera. That led to some really cool stuff. Like, for example, in the opening shot of the film, we're going through a tollbooth and Mike's paying while talking to camera. During the shot, the guy in the tollbooth gave him change. In the middle of his sentence, Mike thanked the guy. It led to a really loose dialogue exchange that felt raw and real (because it was). And that was perfect. We wanted the fourth wall stuff to feel like documentary, completely real. It ended up making the original footage, which was not as raw, work better. For most of the film, everything was on sticks [tripod] or, even if handheld, it had a considered approach – this was the style of the DP for that segment of the film. The new stuff somehow made it work. It really, in a sense, saved the day for us. It made the film much better than it had been at that point. And all of that was the result of limitations.

When I started in this field, it was overwhelming. I would often think, "Oh shit, I'm responsible for this whole big thing, you know?" I only began to get good results when I had my attention on one little thing at a time. The analogy that comes to mind, is climbing Mount Everest. You don't climb Mount Everest in a single bound. It's one step at a time. Taking on climbing the tallest mountain in the world can be over-whelming. If, however, you're attention is on a single step, it's not overwhelming. It's just one little thing to do. And before you know it, that monumental task is a series of bite-sized chunks. And so I encourage people to put their attention on the bite, not the whole chunk.

SHAUN CLARKE

10.3 Interview Excerpts with Shaun Clarke

Shaun Clarke is a Director and Cinematographer whose work in dance film explores how dance can be transformed through the tools of cinema: lenses, light, sound, and editing. His award-winning dance film work has been featured in numerous international and national film festivals, including: the San Francisco Dance Film Festival, Portland Dance Film Festival (OR), the Thomas Edison Film Festival, San Souci Dance Film Festival (Boulder, CO), Screen Dance International (Detroit), the Fine Arts Film Festival (Santa Barbara, CA) the Massachusetts Cultural Council, the University Film and Video Association.[1]

FIGURE SC.1 Still from Lullaby by Shaun Clarke, 2019.

Ingrid Stobbe:
Every artist has a journey of finding their landing spot and the area where they feel, they found a home and expressing themselves could be a genre phase of production that speaks to them in a particularly provocative way. So could you speak to us about your own path and how you feel like you've found your home and it's filmmaking? When you talk through that, perhaps thinking particularly about the twists and turns that maybe it didn't work out that pointed you that way and illuminated your path, especially when it wasn't necessarily visible at that moment, but maybe later on?

Shaun Clarke:
My interest in filmmaking started when I was a kid. I mean, I was nine years old when I first started messing around with cameras. So it's been a long, lifelong interest of mine. And it has definitely evolved since those early days. I mean, I was primarily interested in the technology at first and learning how to use a video camera or a photo camera. And it wasn't until high school really, that I started to see the artistic possibilities of using a camera in a cinema in general and television production.

That interest in high school led me to studying film production as an undergrad. And probably the first big twist was in realizing that I didn't want to be a director. A lot of my interests had grown out of watching fictional narrative feature-length films. And that was the kind of image I had of the standard for artistic achievement and in filmmaking. And

Interviews With Working Artists **131**

so it was a very kind of narrow lens by which I viewed the possibilities with filmmaking. And in particular with being a director, I, when I was in school, I realized my own strengths and my weaknesses, and that being a fictional filmmaking director was not something that I was excited about once I got into the trenches. But I did really love using the camera and the kind of puzzle that came with trying to communicate stories or ideas visually. So halfway through my undergrad I focused primarily on cinematography and I thought of myself as a cinematographer. And so that continued beyond school. And I worked as a freelance cinematographer for years, after that, and still do.

In graduate school, I was kind of forced to think about, my own creative voice and to put together a project where I was a creative lead directing. And after tossing around a lot of ideas, I had decided to just try my hand at working with dance on camera, because I knew that it would align with my strengths as a visual storyteller, and as a cinematographer. In that process of making my first dance film was another epiphany moment for me in terms of what my interests really were. I knew I loved working primarily visually, although I still use sound in the dance pieces. I knew that I loved working with people, and I loved the performance aspect of it. Um, but it was different working with dancers and talking about the way that their bodies were kind of visually being represented on screen versus working with actors and thinking about kind of emotions and things like that. So I did it once for my graduate thesis film, I did it again a few years later, and it just kinda snowballed into this now decades-old interest in practice and doing dance filmmaking and thinking about how I can use my strengths and interests as a filmmaker to transform the present dance performance on the screen.

FIGURE SC.2 Still from Time vs Money by Shaun Clarke, 2014.

Ingrid Stobbe:
Can you talk to us about a project or a collaboration that for you is particularly meaningful, and elaborate what about it was special or of importance to you in your work as an artist in the area that you just talked about - where you find that you best express yourself?

Shaun Clarke:
In 2014 I made a music video slash dance film called *Time Versus Money* by a musical group called The Bynars. And that was the first film project that I was primary creative on, that I made outside of graduate school. I had worked as a cinematographer outside of school, but in terms of like, you know, I want to make a piece I'm going to just do it, no deadlines or expectations – that was the first piece. I just had an idea, I connected with the other artists and we made it happen. So it was important for a number of reasons.

One is I worked with some really talented people on it from the musicians in the band, to the choreographer, to the dancers, to the director of photography, all of the people who helped out. It was a passion project. It was really important to my practice going forward. I found I do need to collaborate with people. I love the collaborative element, and I don't work in a genre that's flooded with resources and money. And so learning how to open myself in the work in a way that it can engage other people, talented people, was super important. It also cemented my interest in dance filmmaking. You know, prior to that, I had made one dance film, I was director, and I worked on a couple of pieces as a cinematographer that focused on dance, but this was starting a trend. So before it was just one point now I have two points, and so it started this like trend line in my creative interests.

Two, it was also really important to initiate work outside of a context where it was expected or required. Learning that I could if I just had an interest in something that I wanted to do, that I could just do it. And that part of becoming an artist seems obvious, but it's actually quite difficult when you consider all of the other demands that we have in our lives and all the other challenges that we have just to like wake up, pay bills, you know, and keep ourselves healthy. So, so, um, so learning to incorporate the artistic practice into my life schedule was important. *And that was the project where I felt like it all kind of fell into place.*

Ingrid Stobbe:
Do you feel this kind of filmmaking pools from other genres particularly strongly? Or do you think that it's sort of its own thing?

Shaun Clarke:
No, it's, it's really its own. I mean, it can bridge different genres that we already know. So, you know, you can have a documentary dance film, you can have a community dance film   You could have experimental dance film, you could have a narrative film that has dance kind of at its core, which is also a form of dance film. And so any, any film where dance is the primary driver of communication, I would

want under that category. So my interest spans across those different genres that can be under the umbrella of dance film as well. I do dance documentary, not as much, but I primarily work with short, short dance performance pieces.

Ingrid Stobbe:
Maya Deren who I love so much, I think her history in dance, there's moments where it's kind of hard to believe that elements of any of her films – there's just an innate connectivity between the cuts that is really physical. And I think that she thought through her body. As opposed to like a million other ways of processing first, I think we all have our strongest muscle we bring that informs our art.

Shaun Clarke:
If I look back at like kind of historical influences, many people who I meet in the dance filmmaking space are dancers or filmmakers, right? So they have the background of dance, that I don't have. I don't, I do not aside from taking tap classes when I was five years old, I never studied dance. So I don't have that background. So that is a significant limitation. I have to work with other people. I am not a choreographer. I'm not a dancer. But I'm going to do dance film. I have to work with other people. It's just baked into my process. So the filmmakers who have done extensive work in dance film are really interesting to me. Maya Deren you know, she has a background as a dancer. She wasn't appearing on screen and some of her dancers like Talley Beatty, *in A Study In Choreography For The Camera,* that's like a foundational influence for me. Hilary Harris has *Nine Variations on a Dance Theme* – foundational for me. That illustrates everything that I'm interested in. How do I transform the dance phrase, the dance performance using the tools of cinema? Then, Norman McLaren who did a lot of animation, but also -

Ingrid Stobbe:
The Pas De Deux!

Shaun Clarke:
Yeah, boom. That, *Ballet Adagio,* which is very, very simple. I mean, it's just a camera filming on stage, but it's in slow motion. And so every move is accentuated And then the other one was *Narcissus,* which is a little more freewheeling in its length. Also really strong.

Ingrid Stobbe:
Can you speak a bit about the on set collaborative process between cinematographer and dancer, and where those two skillsets meet without stepping on one another and inadvertently limiting each other's craft in the process?

Shaun Clarke:
It creates some interesting dynamics in the collaboration. Because I am pushing for what I'm looking for as a filmmaker, right? When that is budding up against what the dancer choreographer is seeing, I am not going to just steamroll them. Like if I, if I have a disagreement with Daniel, Jacob, the camera operator, and I know in my heart that

we're going to do it this way, I just disagree with him. I can confidently say like, all right, we're not going to do that because I know enough about the space. We just have a disagreement. I'm going to make the choice when it comes to the dancers, the choreographers, if they're like, no, we cannot do this, I defer to their expertise in a way. And I'll say, all right, well, you have the dance background. It creates interesting set dynamics that have changed over time because I've work with people multiple years and I kind of have a better rapport than when I'm working with someone for the first time. I'm like you are the expert in this area. I'm the expert in this area. We need to find some way for it to come together because it doesn't work if it's just I film, you dance. It's the concept of the interwoven.

FIGURE SC.3 Still from *SHE/I* by Shaun Clarke, 2020.

Ingrid Stobbe:
Alright, so my last official question today for you is, do you ever find yourself deliberately placing restrictions, or brackets on yourself in your work? Or causing production timelines you have to intentionally meet?

Shaun Clarke:
Yes, I do it as a way of forcing myself to grow as an artist. So if I know that there's something that I feel uncomfortable doing, I frequently set up restrictions that force me to do that. It can be as specific as the type of lenses that I use, if I feel like I'm using too many you know, telephoto close-up shots of the film, I might say, all right, well, I'm going to just shoot this film with a 14-millimeter lens, see what I can get, so then I will have had the experience of doing that. Or when it comes to editing, if I feel like I'm doing too much, montage editing I'm going to have shots that are no shorter than seven seconds or something like that. And so I frequently employ those kinds of restrictions on myself to force myself to grow. When I play music, I frequently heard musicians talk

about, like, you got to force yourself to play stuff that you don't know or force yourself to do things. So I usually do that with, with any film project I'm working on. I mean, whether I'm working on a dance film as a director or films that I'm working as a cinematographer I always build them in, because it also helps me make sense of what to do.

When the possibilities are endless, sometimes it's hard to make a decision versus adding even that one restriction, which can then force you to try to either work around it or work with it. And that allows for almost like an entree into making all the other decisions, to find yourself. Sometimes those limitations are thrust upon people, right? So if you have just one location and you have 10 minutes to get a shot, and you have this one light or so, like, those limitations become built in based off of your resources, but from the outset of a project, I'm constantly thinking about some of those other creative limitations that I can place on myself that are going to force me to see things differently or to try new things.

FIGURE SC.4 Still from *The Perfect Dancer* by Shaun Clarke, 2019.

OLIVER CURTIS

10.4 Interview Excerpts with Oliver Curtis

One of the youngest cinematographers ever to be invited to join the British Society of Cinematographers (BSC), Oliver Curtis began his photographic education studying photography, then went on to study film and television at the London College of Printing. Afterwards he directed numerous documentaries for Channel Four and BBC TV before moving fully into cinematography with such feature films as The Wedding Date, Death At A

Funeral (original), *Unrelated*, and *Last Night In Soho*, for which he provided additional cinematography. He's also done long-form television work for platforms such as Netflix and Apple+ shows and even experimental gallery-based installations. He's also in demand for commercials for such high-profile clients as Pantene, Coca-Cola, Sony, and many more. Oliver also continues to produce photographic work; his first solo exhibition *Volte-Face* premiered at London's Royal Geographical Society, and a book of the project is published by Dewi Lewis Publishing.

I took a year off after college before going to university, and explored my photographic interests during that year. I came to New York in 1983, took a lot of photographs. I just walked the streets, had no money, took pictures of graffiti. I found those by Keith Haring, Basquiat, and all those guys on the walls. At the time I didn't know who they were, I was just interested in what I saw. I really enjoyed that. Then I went to film school in back London.

This was pre-digital, so all the other students tended to use me as their Director of Photography (DoP) because I knew how to use a light meter and I wasn't afraid to expose film. So while I was always shooting for other people, I still thought of myself as sort of a budding director. I came out of college not knowing what I was going to do. So I kind of did both – I carried on shooting for other people and also directing. I got into directing documentaries for broadcast as I had a few lucky breaks. It was a very strange time where I was getting opportunities to be a full-fledged DoP, not really knowing what I was doing, but somehow getting away with it. I had never worked as a assistant, as a focus puller, or loader.

The cinematography work was getting bigger and bigger in scale and I did my first indie feature film. As my second feature film was shaping up, *Love and Death on Long Island,* and I thought "Do I really want to do this, to be a cinematographer. What about my directing?" The director said, "Look, let's go and scout Long Island and see how you feel". At the same time, I took the opportunity to do a cinematography workshop in Rockport in Maine, which was two weeks of intensive talking, thinking, sleeping cinematography." In Rockport, the course leader said that unfortunately one of the DoP teachers couldn't come, but they had a replacement from the UK called Jack Cardiff. Jack was like the God of cinematography to me. He had an Oscar for *The Red Shoes*, he shot *Matter of Life and Death*, my favorite film. He shot *Black Narcissus*. I couldn't believe my luck. Today it would be like having Roger Deakins suddenly turn up. One of the legends, a multiple Oscar winner who had shot the old three strip Technicolor process like it had never been shot before, just beautiful, beautiful images. So I was fortunate enough to spend two weeks with this guy, one of the greats, talking film, asking questions. I remember getting to the end of one day totally immersed in this world, then walking out in the Maine countryside. The low afternoon autumnal light was striking a silver birch tree. It kind of glowed, took on its own life because of the backlighting. And I looked at this thing almost like as a biblical apparition! I thought: cinematography – that's it, that's what I'm doing and you can't do it part time, it's too frigging difficult to do part time. I'm either going to do that or direct, because you can't do both. At least, that's what I felt. I thought, "Okay, I'm going to have to really go for this." So I stopped taking the directing gigs and really focused on being a cinematographer. And the rest sort of, as they say, is history.

I would have been the world's worst assistant. I don't have the temperament for it. And one thing I still do when I start a new show and I get my crew together, I explain to them, "Guys, you see before you somebody who's never done your job. I know what your job is and I know as a DoP what I need on set. I respect what you do because these are jobs I personally could not do. But I do know what I need from the team as a whole." It's a team with really specific skill sets that all meld together. We're there to serve the vision of the director.

One thing about camera operating is that you get pretty focused on the frame. And when you step away from operating, you tend to light in a more broad brushstroke fashion. You light the space rather than the frame. And the reason that's good is that it's particularly useful if the actors don't necessarily go where you expected them to go. You may also have multiple cameras trained on a space, so actually you have to light multiple frames. In stepping back from the single composition, you have to think about all of the lenses, and all of the space and what the light's doing in that space. I find I can do that better by not being sat on the dolly and I can take more of a global view. I also find myself being more useful to the directors than I would be if I was having to deal with the mechanics of camera motion and framing and so on. Some DoP's prefer to operate. Everyone has their own way of doing things.

There's a phrase we say when you put a camera on a tripod: it's called Comfortable Working Height (CWH). People put the tripod up, put a head on it, and put the camera and it's usually at eye level. That's the easiest place to work on the lens and the other accessories and it just happens to be the comfortable working height. But is it the right place for the shot? You'd be surprised how many scenes are shot at a CWH, where the style of the scene is dictated by the habits of a camera operator. But you have to shake people out of that notion, force them to think, "where the best place to tell this story? It might be higher or lower, is it really at C.W.H.?"

I don't see myself as an artist – I'm a craftsman. In my stills photographic practice, that's where I could be an artist, where I'm just doing my own thing. Film-making is much more of a collaborative process and you're in a team. It's difficult to say that I get to express my own vision in a film or tv show. Each show is a new experience. It's a new dance every time you work with a new director. And each director has different footwork, you know, different steps. And that's the joy of it. It really is the collaboration. So it's not that I would define myself as an artist, but I work in an artistic practice, but collaboratively with other artists.

The challenge these days is that people consume films in so many different ways. You see people on the subway watching on a phone, people with an iPad, as well as sitting at home in front of the TV. So the work we do has to function in so many different environments and in all of those environments the framing, the color, contrast, and the brightness can all have a different impacts, positive or negative. If you shoot everything too close and watch it on a big TV, it might be suffocating. But you're watching things on an iPhone, a wide shot with tiny details, as in *Fargo* or something like that, it could get lost. So you can't win, really. The only thing you can do is just be true to your intent – do what's right for the storytelling.

Some years ago I was on an American show that shot in the UK and then finished in the US. And it was really out there stylistically, very bold. I remember chatting to one of the network executives, and I said, "I'm so impressed that you're letting the show be as daring as it can be: dark and moody, really quirky." And he said to me, "There is just so much product out there that unless you make it distinctive, it's going to disappear. We want and need it to be distinctive." That is an interesting dilemma. They don't want to alienate audiences if it's too dark, or has unusual lensing, or whatever. But at the same time it's got to be memorable and distinctive – make the audience want to come back for more. You sometimes get the complete opposite where your aesthetic choices are considered too challenging, such as using a wide aspect ratio that requires narrower letterboxing (i.e., 2.35:1). Much depends on the particular network executives you happen to get. But when they are really bold visually ... think of *Breaking Bad*, or *Better Call Saul*, of *Godless*, the new generation of TV shows, that's where they succeed: not watering the visuals down, not trying to pander to the common denominator. They succeed because they are true to themselves and they have a vision and they stick to it. But not every show is like that.

A project that was meaningful to me ... inevitably I'm going to say *Death At a Funeral* directed by Frank Oz. I came to that after a series of experiences that were really tough. I had been struggling with my craft for quite a while, through a series of jobs that were unsatisfactory and stressful. I was losing the joy of the craft. And then I met Frank. I had an interview with him and it turned out he had gone through a similar experience in recent years, coming off the big-budget remake of *The Stepford Wives*. *Death At a Funeral* was a much smaller production. I think from the moment we met there was a kind of,

"Let's just go have fun, right?". You know, "We have a brilliant, playful script. We have a ridiculously great cast. What's not to like?". We were going to craft the very best movie we could possibly make, but also we were going to bloody well enjoy doing it! We both came into that film with that mindset and it showed, I think. You only have to look at the behind-the-scenes outtake reels to sense the joy of everyone involved. Every day was joy, pretty much, and that's what got me in back in love with the film-making process. I think before that film I had forgotten that it's a privilege to do what we do for a living. I had begun to take it all too seriously, it had become a dark cloud. But on *Death At a Funeral* it was just like, I can't wait for tomorrow!

That film needed to be about performance first and foremost; let the actors' performance breathe, let the frame breathe, prioritize the comedic beat. The cinematography was there to serve the needs of the comedic performances. I tried to light the film in that frame of mind, with the right kind of sensibility. It's so important to get to be connected with the spirit of a show and with the spirit of a director.

A producer friend for a big, new American show shooting in the UK called me looking for a DoP to do reshoots for multiple episodes. The series clearly had story problems they were trying to fix. It had big ensemble cast, very experienced players. High production values, a lot of VFX. But despite many weeks of reshooting, the problems remained and the show didn't get recommissioned. "It's the script, stupid" someone once said. And I believe that's true. It doesn't matter how much money you throw at it visually, it's not going to compensate if the character's motivations don't make sense or there are great holes in the narrative. So in the end they didn't need a DoP to come in and do additional photography – they needed to start again with new writing. It's the story, stupid.

"Fix it in prep." It's a good adage for students (as it is for everyone) – you just say to them, "Listen, you think the problems start when you're shooting – the problems start when you're preparing. If you don't consider what could happen, you need to think what you want to happen – think about what's required down the line. The more you do that, the more prepared you are to deal with it and make a success of what you're trying to do." You often hear this phrase, "We'll fix it in post." But more than anything else, you fix it in prep. So whenever we talk about the pre-production schedule on a show I will push for as much prep as I can get. It just gives you a better chance of delivering on budget and is also creatively more satisfying. It means when things don't go to plan, you're better prepared for how you solve it. But without the prep, if something doesn't go to plan it's much harder to work a way round it.

The more prep you've done, the more prepared you are for the unexpected. If you don't have the prep, the chances are you're going to be sort of hamstrung. Wherever possible, I like to build in some thinking time – a surprisingly rare commodity in the film and TV business! Just to have a location or studio build to yourself for a while, even a few minutes, might allow you to come up with an interesting approach or solution you might otherwise miss. Thinking time may be considered a luxury, but actually it's a necessity.

There are a lot of directors who want to leave chance as a big element. "Positive accidents" as they call it, "Let's see what happens." This can lead to really exciting results in performance and in image making. But the key to being ready for this approach is thorough prep. Building up your skills to allow for the unexpected, honing your instincts. The less prep you have, the more you winging it and the chances are you're going to be governed by circumstances rather than the other way round.

Edgar Wright is a very prepared director, so to work with him you've got to be really prepared; everybody raises their game to work alongside him. And so I got a great buzz from that. I was doing some second unit work on *Last Night In Soho* for them and the shoot went long, and the original DoP, Chung-hoon Chung, had to leave. So I took over the main unit, but then COVID struck and it shut down. So we had a generous amount of prep once we restarted. I watched the existing footage multiple times, talked to the chief lighting technician, talked to the production designer, and made sure that all the lighting and lensing would blend with the existing footage and the scenes that we were going to do fresh. The gaffer and the camera department had fantastic records of what they did which helped enormously. Edgar likes to have another go at scenes he doesn't feel are quite working. His producers are also great filmmakers; very respectful and supportive of everybody. So even though I wasn't the principal DoP on the picture, I found it very satisfying creatively.

Many years ago I shot a period drama for the BBC. The director was really challenging. In one scene we had two characters go into a completely dark room – no practicals [existing lights], no candles, no motivated light of any sort. The director also said he didn't want movie-stye moonlight coming in the window. I thought, "How do I light this?" I was still quite green at that time and quite inexperienced – dark, moody scenes were one of the biggest challenges. Despite doing my best, I thought, "Damn, this is dark. This is too dark." But we shot it and moved on. I thought, "Oh, well, I'll never work again." When the show was broadcast I called my mother and I said, "What did you think of the episode?" She said, "I loved it." "What about that scene where those guys go into that really dark room? You know, don't you think it was too dark?" "Oh, I love that," she said. "I loved the atmosphere in that room, you listened to what they were saying, you know. I was riveted by it." I learned a lesson that night: it's not all about what you can see – sometimes it's about what you don't see, it's about sound, and it's about mood. People see and feel other things, not necessarily exactly what we might anticipate or plan for.

I think that's the key takeaway: try to be as prepared as possible for the unexpected, whatever it is. The more prep you do, the more successful your improvised response will be.

PETE DOCTER

10.5 Interview Excerpts with Pete Docter

Pete Docter's interest in animation began at the age of eight when he created his first flipbook. He went on to study character animation at the California Institute of the Arts in Valencia, CA where he produced a variety of short films, one of which won a Student Academy Award®. Starting at Pixar in 1990 as the studio's third animator, Docter helped develop Toy Story, Pixar's first full-length animated feature film, for which he also was supervising animator. He also wrote initial story treatments for both Toy Story 2 and WALL.E. Docter eventually became the Oscar®-winning director of his own movies Monsters, Inc., Up, Inside Out, and Soul. He is also the Chief Creative Officer at Pixar Animation Studios.

A lot of people, when I tell them, "I work at Pixar," they say, "It must be nice to have infinite money and time." Well, guess what? We don't. Jonas Rivera (who produced *Up* and *Inside Out*) made the observation that if you have five months to make a movie, it will take exactly five months to finish. If you have five years to make a movie, you'll use the five years. Somehow it always takes whatever time you have available. That's because it's human nature to push up right to the edges of what you have. So I think it's really important to have parameters.

In our process, it actually takes five years to make a Pixar movie. Five years is a long time, so we set a bunch of interim deadlines for ourselves. In six months, we're going to have the whole thing up on pre-viz reels, and we're going to show other people. And we've booked the screening room, and invited people to watch. That gives you pressure, because, "Uh-oh, I'm going to have to show it to Andrew Stanton or Brad Bird or John Lasseter or whoever, and we've got to show them *something*!" And that really drives a lot. As much as I'd like to think, "I'm totally responsible, I don't need deadlines," or conversely, "I can't have a deadline, I need the freedom for inspiration to hit," it always ends up that the best ideas come out of the pressure of a deadline. Yeah … [laughs] I hate that.

I love that story of Spielberg on *Jaws* and the shark not working. Half the shots they wanted they couldn't get. So they had to resort to showing ways to imply the shark instead of seeing it – which of course is way more scary.

There's a similar story I heard about *Jurassic Park*. The character Nedry was supposed to be followed by a dilophosaurus as his jeep is caught in the mud. But the puppet wasn't working, and the technical artists said we're going to have to fix the thing and come back to shoot it next week. Apparently, Spielberg said, "No, we're going to get this today," and came up with the idea that every time Nedry looks back, the dinosaur is just positioned closer behind him. Every time he looks back, it's moved closer. So smart! Again, a restriction nobody would want, but it made for a better scene.

We had some heavy restrictions with *Toy Story*. Given the state of the technology back then, we could barely do anything. Hair, clothes, anything organic, was very difficult. Everything looked like plastic. So we thought, *Well, let's take advantage of that and make our characters plastic!* And so: *Toys*. John Lasseter and the team had done that short film, "*Tin Toy*", [1988 Pixar short featuring a tin toy being shaken by a baby] which set the table. But, you know, the weakness of that film I always felt was the baby, because it's got this horrifying kind of look. Though I guess it kind of works for the story because maybe that's what a toy would feel from their point of view, right? That the sweet baby is actually kind of a little monster. So back to *Toy Story*, we knew we needed to limit our view of humans. Interestingly, if we had been able to do humans really well, we might have told the story differently – and maybe not as well! That limitation kept the focus on the toys, who were the characters we wanted the audience to connect with anyway. It makes us experience the whole story more from the toys' point of view. Which is really what's important.

It's really expensive and difficult to draw or build human characters. It just takes more time ... they're always tricky. Disney's animated *Cinderella* (1951) is an exercise in avoiding showing humans, for that same reason. They told most of the story through the mice, to avoid having to draw people – and once again, that restriction probably resulted in a better movie.

There were a bunch of limitations on *Toy Story*. Anything organic was super expensive. Even today it's somewhat difficult. As an example, we had this thing where Sid was burning a hole in Woody's forehead by using a magnifying glass. And in the storyboards, Woody runs and dunks his head in the dog's water bowl to cool it off. We thought it was funny. But the technical team was like, "No, no, no, water is way expensive. We can't do water!" So we're thinking, *How do we get around this*? So we took the camera and lowered it so you couldn't see what was in the bowl. And then we made it a bowl of Fruit Loops instead. So instead of water splashing out, you just have a few pieces of cereal. Much easier. And as a bonus, the animator came up with a gag that when Woody brings his head up, he has two cereal loops stuck to his eyes. So it ended up being even better than water, you know? So all those kind of restrictions that make your brain go into overdrive: "Oh, geez, OK, how do I get around this? How can I still get what I need?"

On *Monsters Inc.*, I remember thinking: OK, this guy, Sulley, the main character that we're following, he has to be both scary and appealing. And I couldn't visualize how to do that unless he had fur. Fur gives you that softness. Even if you can't touch it, you touch it with your eyes, and it feels soft and approachable like a cat or dog. I knew if Sulley had, say, lizard skin, it would be a little off-putting, and would make it a lot harder to really empathize with this guy. Well, we had never done fur, especially dynamic fur. If you go back and look at *Toy Story 1* and *2*, any hair is basically a rigid form with a fuzzy texture on it. It barely moves, and when it does, the animators had to hand-position and move the hair in large clumps. With Sulley, we knew his hair was going to have it be dynamic; when he moves his arms, the fur overlaps without animators needing to move thousands of strands. How would we do that? We had no idea. But instead of saying, "No, Pete, we can't do it," the studio said, "Okay, we're going to make this happen. We're going to buy this small company that's done research in computer simulation, and hire new people." We developed a whole new step within our existing process to be able to do fur. And even then, it was so expensive, computationally, they told us we could only have one character with fur in any given shot. We got kind of creative there. There are some characters that are more or less rigid surface but with fur in certain areas, like a fur necklace or fur on their head or whatever. So we kind of stretched the rules a bit. The results were worth it. People still tell me how amazed they were by that fur when the film came out. The studio recognized this was a chance to do something new.

We've calculated over the years that if you have more cuts, it's more expensive. Every time you set up the camera in a different place, set up lights and so on, there's an investment of time. So, we've often given ourselves this restriction: "OK, we have to tell this chunk of the story in no more than 20 shots. In the storyboards we had 50 shots. How can we tell the same story with fewer shots?" And man, somehow that restriction produces some great visuals!

Length is another restriction. A lot of times our early story reels (animatics) will be 110 or 120 minutes. But with animation every second on screen is thousands of dollars, literally! We can't afford to animate 120 minutes! So, you have to tell that same story in 85 or 90 minutes. And again, it's always a better movie. I've never watched a movie and said, "It was good, but I wish it was longer." On the other hand, I don't know how many times I've looked at the first cut of something and it's so long and boring and rambling. And then, when you have the discipline of forcing yourself to cut it down, it gets better. I think what happens is that you realize, "If I can only keep what's truly important, which ideas will stay? I really love this idea, but with a gun to my head I realize it really doesn't have anything to do with the main thing I want the audience to track." So length restrictions force you to get rid of anything unessential.

And showing your work to people as you go is important. I know that a lot of students or other people think, "No, no, it's not done. I'm going to finish it first and *then* I'll show you, and you'll see how glorious and genius it all is." And inevitably if you do that, you've invested all this time only to have people say, "What's going on? I don't understand this, it doesn't make any sense." So as painful as it is, forcing yourself to show other people along the way, it's a way to give yourself perspective, to see it as your audience will. We have it built into our system to show our work to each other at about 12 different times along the way. In outline form, and script, and then at eight to ten different screenings. We show it to each other which allows us to see it ourselves with fresh eyes.

At Cal Arts, where I went to school, everyone made their own short films every year. The first-year student films were purposely not allowed to have sound. Part of that was because, well, that's a whole other technical bunch of gunk that you got to learn. But more importantly, it forced us to rely on visuals to tell the story. And of course, students don't like that. "I want sound! I'm not going to be able to do this without sound effects, or music. Waaa!" But guess what? The films come out better with that restriction.

I think there's an illusion that people have: they think there are some people who are just geniuses who, when they think of an idea, it just appears finished in their head, and all they've got to do is shoot that and it's brilliant. Truth is, when you make something it always evolves and changes and grows, even as you're in the middle of making things. In my experience, tenacity trumps talent. If you have the persistence and determination to keep hammering at it, and the clarity to see whether it's getting better or worse, that's really the name of the game.

The directing job is very confusing to people who've never done it. The job is to make a great movie. "OK, well, it's Monday. What do I today? It's going to be four years before the movie is done; what do I do tomorrow?" I feel like the first thing you're looking for is, first, the "hook": what's going to make me interested and engaged with the situation and characters right at the beginning? And then second, where am I going? What's my – I guess I call it the emotional punch line – by the end of the movie? Usually late in act two or act three, there's some scene that makes my spine tingle and affects me emotionally. In *Inside Out*, it's Joy in the dump, and her realization that sadness actually leads to happiness. Usually this scene comes right after the low point, where everything is lost and the character is totally screwed. And then there's some sort of epiphany that happens, that causes the character to see things in a new way. And that's what I'm searching for early on. You find those two anchors: something interesting about the concept that makes me engage from the beginning, and make me want to watch, and then I know it's going to lead to something that's going to make people emotionally connect and relate. We will work on all the other stuff for years. But if I have those two starting out, I'm in pretty good shape. I don't really care what happens at the very end. We can work that out. It takes a while to arrive at something truly satisfying. Every film I've worked on it has had five or six different endings at the very least. In terms of the very end. But the emotional thing, the epiphany is more important. That's hard to come by, I feel.

As for your last question, if there was one limitation I could have whisked away, never again have to deal with, what would it be? Hmmm. Well, I could easily answer, "I wish I could get rid of my insecurity and have more confidence," but probably, in the end, it's made my work better. The fact that I stop to question myself and have self-doubts is also what makes me pursue other people's voices and loop in other points of view. Which makes the work better. It feels like everything – at least that I can think of off the top of my head – everything that I've thought of as a negative at the time, when I look back at it, was actually kind of a positive.

GRETCHEN HALL

10.6 Interview Excerpts with Gretchen Hall

Gretchen Hall earned her BA from Fordham University and her MFA from New York University's acclaimed Graduate Acting program. She has performed on and off Broadway and regionally at such theaters as A.C.T, The Old Globe, Shakespeare Theatre Company, Arena Stage, among many others, and internationally, with NYU's The Continuum Company in Italy. Her television credits include, to list a few, FBI, The Blacklist, Person of Interest, Gossip Girl, and Law & Order. In film, she garnered a "Best Actress in a Short Film" award for the title role in "Cammy", and was featured in such films as The Weekend and Almost in Love. She currently teaches at Indiana University and lives in Bloomington, IN with her husband and three amazing daughters.

I knew I wanted to be an actress starting in fifth grade. My mom was a social worker and then she got a degree in psychiatric epidemiology and she worked with bipolar patients in the New York Psychiatric Institute, and she encountered some really interesting people, celebrities and people in states of mania. So starting around maybe ten or eleven, my mom would tell me these stories about her patients. And I loved the stories so much. I decided at the time, "Well, I know I love these stories so much – I either want to be my mom or I want to be the patient." And then my mom taught us Lady Macbeth's "Out damn spot" speech. My sister, who's nine and I'm eleven, were walking through our house going, "Out damn spot, out I say!" And I just loved it and loved this idea, "Oh, my gosh, you can pretend to be crazy. It's so fun." And so that stuck.

I knew I wanted to go to New York City. My parents had lived there and so there was this exoticism. And I was born in New York, but I'd never spent any time there. I actually went for one year at Indiana University because I missed the deadline for New York University. So my freshman year at IU, I applied to NYU and I went to Chicago for the audition. And in retrospect, I know I was really terrible. I know I was just shouting and I thought volume and anger equaled really good acting. And, I'm a little like, embarrassed looking back on it now. But I didn't have any real training or anything. So, I didn't get into NYU. But I did get into Fordham University and I got a scholarship, so I went to Fordham at the Lincoln Center campus right in the center of things. It was like, "Wow, I'm in New York City." It was just the coolest. And I really loved my time there, loved all my teachers and my classmates.

Then I graduated and spent three years working as an actor/waiter/babysitter or whatever I could to get my hands on money. And I did the Renaissance Faire in Sterling, New York. It's one of the top ones – you spend a month rehearsing and playing games and figuring out your character. The people there are really fun. Then I came back after the Fair and worked at the theme restaurant Dr. Jekyll and Mr. Hyde. I saw in Backstage you could get your Actors Equity [union] card by being a waitress there. And so I went and I auditioned and I just had this whole summer of creating a character. So I created this British maid and I came in and I got it and the guy said, "Look, you get your Actors Equity card right away – I just ask that you stick around for at least three months." And I was like, "Okay." And it was so dark. Who knows what the restaurant actually looks like if the lights were on. And I had to push this old carriage with a baby that would pop out. And I remember at one point pulling the trigger [to pop the baby up] and it crushed my finger, like it broke my finger, and I didn't tell my parents or anything. And I was like, "This place is the worst." So three months ends, and I was, "I gotta get out of here." I held my promise. Got my Actors Equity card. And I got out of there.

During that time, I would do anything I could to act. It was all free. Like, I mean, free-free. I would do student films with New York Film Academy – never saw one of those films, ever. And then I also worked with grad students at Columbia University. The Columbia directing students would work with professional actors. Those directors are huge now, like, Saheem Ali. I was his go-to girl for most of his scenes. And now he's a New York Public Theater director. It was an education for me. And through those three years, I was like, "I see where I want to be, and I know I'm not there, so I need more training." And part of it was that I needed more training but part of it was also that I saw what was happening to people who get an NYU MFA and I saw what happened to their career and that's where I want to be. So I applied.

At the time, I was a waitress at Times Square Brewery, which is like now where Sephora is on Times Square. So the subway steps come up in front of the window that was our cocktail lounge area. So this day I'd had my interview with NYU, had my auditions, and I was like, "I know I'm going to get in. I can just feel it." So I knew. I was confident. I don't know if I've ever been that confident since then, but I was like, "I know I belong here. I know you want me. I know I'm good. You're going to accept me." So afterwards I was working near the Brewery window when I recognized a first-year NYU graduate theater student who had been at a question and answer session I had to do that morning coming up the steps of the subway. And I knocked on the window and I was like, "Hey, here, come, I want to say hi." And he came in and he was, "Well, how did your interview go?" And I said, "I'm almost positive I'm going to get an offer." So he said, "Okay, here's what you do – they're going to call you. They're going to give you an offer and they're going to give you money and you say, 'Thank you, I need more.'" And it was like, "Really?" And he's, "Yes, just trust me. They aren't going to turn you down because you want money." And I have never done this before, but I was like, "Okay." So Zelda Fichandler (former chair and artistic director of the NYU Grad Acting program) called me and she said, "We'd like to offer you a spot. We can offer you like a quarter off your tuition." I was like, "Oh, thank you so much. I'm so excited. I do need more money, though." And I did that two times. They called me back and they offered me more. I was like, "Oh, my gosh, thank you so much. I still need it. I just this is going to be tough for me because I don't have any support and I'm busting my ass to be a waitress here in the city." And so they called back a third time and Zelda was like, "Are you sitting down?" And I was walking in an alleyway on MacDougal Street and I sat down on the curb and I was, "Yes, now I'm sitting." She's like, "We want to offer you a full ride." And I would not have done it if it were not for that student! Honestly, the first call they would have made, I would have said, "Yes, thank you, this is the top school. I'll take it."

As for my acting itself, there is no plan. And I think for most actors, there is no plan. I go into each production not knowing because you don't know who your cast mates are. You have to go in and ... I go in and have to be adaptable to the director's style.

And then there's so many different types of actors out there. But one thing about the way I work is it's very spontaneous, so I respond in the moment. I remember I was working with a younger actress and I remember her saying, "I always get a little ... not anxious, but like excited during our scene because I never know what you're going to do." Now, I always did the same movement, physical movement. I was baking bread or some vegetables or something. So if she did something or if I had a moment of like a memory of whatever that's connected to the character, you know, there was a different kind of energy, but it was all like ... I think if a typical audience member were to watch it three different times, they might see the same thing. They may not necessarily pick up on the nuance, but this actress said, "It just feels different every time." And I was like, "Yeah, I know." [Laughs.] But she was young, and I know when I was 22 year old, I was like, "I don't know … how do I itch my nose here? Like, I feel nervous even doing that. How do people have human behavior in front of a camera or audience?" And through training, it should feel spontaneous. So that's why it's hard to answer that question, to say, "I'm going to go in and it's going to be like this."

An actress has to be vulnerable, but you develop this other part of you that's tougher, like just a little tougher that says, "Look, I'm going to try this and maybe it will work or maybe it won't." So being okay with failure is important, although I don't think it's necessarily failure. So I try to be, when a director asks for something else, I try to be like, "Yeah, okay, cool. Yeah. Okay, let me try something else." And I think I approach that in the audition room too. That's why I love auditions, because it's my chance to try and show, "This is how I see the character." And if I have a director who is able to see that I'm an intelligent person, hopefully the way they work is, "Okay, she presented this – obviously she can do something else." Not all directors can do that, right? They think I bring in this character and that's all I can do. But there have been moments where I bring in something and I'm like, "I think this is how I see the character." And they're like, "Well, why don't you try this?" And that can be a little, "Okay, okay, I'm not terrible. They're just asking me to do something different." And if I can approach it with that mindset, then it creates a more creative environment. If I come in and I'm like, "Oh, but no – this is how I saw her," then obviously we're not the right fit. Right? So I think through a lot of being willing to have egg on my face, I don't really care about failing. And if I don't get it, I don't get it. And it'll hurt a little bit, but, like, just try something. And then when it's successful is when a director sees that, like, "Well, she's got something. What if we tried this instead," then it's a collaborative process, a give and take.

I was cast in a *Law and Order* episode. I auditioned and I was like, "I nailed that and I should definitely get an offer." And I did. Then we were filming the scene I auditioned with, but now there was a huge set full of people, including actors I admired. And I was very nervous and I couldn't bring it to the level that I had in the audition room, which was very vulnerable, weepy, crying. I just couldn't get it. And the director pulled me aside, he was like, "I need you to do what you did in the audition." And I was. "Oh, of course." But, you know, already I'm like, "I know you need that – I just can't get there right now." And I was just … I couldn't. And then what I did was I said, "I just need 5 minutes." And I went and I hid underneath a table. Here's this conference room set with all these people, I don't even know where the camera was, and I just was like, "I need 5 minutes." So they shut everything down for 5 minutes. And I went and underneath the table and I just sat there and I put in my headphones and then listened to this emo music and got to this very vulnerable place. And I came out and I was like, "Okay, I'm ready." And I did it on the first take. So what you see is the first take after that moment. So in my mind, there's some success in that. I was confident enough to say, "I need 5 minutes to give you what you want," and shut down production. But in other ways it wasn't a success because this director didn't give me any direction to help me. He just said, "I want you to do what you did before." And so I was in this place trying to recreate a moment, which never works for an actor.

The pre-interview questionnaire asked, "Was there a project or collaboration that was particularly meaningful to you? And I know, like, how dumb for me to say *"Cammy"* [short film written & directed by Pace starring Gretchen, for which she won a Best Actress award] talking to you, but it really was. I liked it because it made me, as the actor part, of the collaboration, which I think happens in theater, but less so in film. And so I felt like you and I came at it as a team, coming up with the idea. And then you went to your creative world and created this beautiful piece. But it felt really fun to have some sort of say in that. And then I liked collaborating with you as the director. And there really is that relationship of, like, you're telling me what to do and, or asking me or offering guidance, and me, like, "Yeah, okay." And like, sometimes I would buck against it and sometimes I would be like, "Oh, yeah, I didn't … . Like what? What is that? Oh, yeah. Okay, let me try that."

William Pace:
I would say *"Cammy"* was one of the most fun films I've done. From the get-go it was collaborative – me asking you, after you had that bad experience on the set of that TV show, "What do you want to play? I'll write a part for you – what do you want to do?" And of all the things in the world you could say, you tell me that off-the-wall thing about wanting to cough blood into a handkerchief. I was like … "Uh, ohhh … kay." And from there it just kinda kept rolling. Like, once it got out we were going to make a film together, [actress] Sam [Dyar] comes in my office, asks, "You got a part for me?" I go, "What can you do?" "I can tap dance." "No, this is a drama, what am I going to do with …" Pause. Gears started whirring in my head. Then … "You know what – okay. Yeah. Let's do that. You're in." And that single moment then became the entire background of your character – suddenly I knew Cammy was a dance instructor and that her husband had had an affair with one of her students. And that moment is some people's favorite moment, when those two young women come in tapdancing out of the blue in a medical center. It was all kind of, "I don't know if this will work, but let's try it." It felt very open from the very beginning. It created that kind of collaborative experience you always hear films are supposed to be, but rarely are.

Gretchen Hall:
And seeing the way that one day when [producer] Tom [Rondinella] kicked that crew member out for making an inappropriate comment after a take. It made me feel protected as an actor, because [co-actor] Deirdre Yates and were feeling very vulnerable. When Tom kicked her out it felt like, "Okay. This is a professional set. Everyone must behave professionally and we need to be treated professionally as well." And I love that moment, that feeling of being taken care of by the creative team. That's what actors want.

FRANK OZ

10.7 Interview Excerpts with Frank Oz

Following in his parents' puppeteering footsteps, Frank Oz's young talent was noticed by Jim Henson, who persuaded Oz to come work with him and became integral to the development of The Muppets, creating many famous Muppet characters. Oz also worked with George Lucas creating Yoda in the original Star Wars and has performed Yoda in all subsequent appearances. He began film directing as co-director with Henson on The Dark Crystal and has since directed over a dozen films, including, Little Shop of Horrors, Dirty Rotten Scoundrels, Bowfinger, The Score, Death at a Funeral, and the documentary Muppet Guys Talking. He has also directed theater, including In and Of Itself, whose film version he also directed.

The most important thing about limitations for me first, for a director, is that if you don't have any, there's no "juice". If you want to be a director, a journeyman director, anybody can do that: learn the film language, learn the shots, learn the lenses, you know, anybody can do that. If that's the kind of director you want to be and stay on budget exactly, and stay on schedule exactly and just shoot what you're supposed to, what the script says, OK ... but there's no juice in there, you know? And the restrictions, the "No – you don't have that much time." "No – the sun's going down." "No – the actor's sick today." "No – the crane is missing a part." "No ..." It goes on and on and on. That's when the juice occurs. That's it. "Holy shit, what are we gonna do?" And that's where the fun happens. That's filmmaking to me. The other stuff is good craft, but the filmmaking is the juice and the excitement, saying, "Holy fuck. Hey, how about this!?" That's the joy.

I do believe in order to get to that place, one really has to learn the craft first, and then, if you do get stuck and have restrictions, you have a toolbox of craft you can rely on and those tools can help you create your way out. But if you don't have that craft, if all you have is an idea, you can't go further with it. But again, the joy of directing is getting caught in some kind of corner and boxing your way out of it with talented people. And then all of a sudden, that just creates something you never thought would happen and it's fantastic!

Take Orson Welles – the studio didn't want him for *A Touch of Evil*, but because Charlton Heston was the star and he wanted Orson to direct, he got to direct. But they were afraid he was going to go over budget and they gave him restrictions to make sure he didn't. So he had like, I don't know, 12 pages, eight pages to shoot or something and on the very first day of the shoot, the very first day of shooting, he planned and shot the shoebox scene. It's like a dance where he did it in one long take in two or three rooms and instead of getting a close-up then cutting to another close-up, the actors came to the camera to make it close. It's exquisite. It's choreography. It's beautiful. He rehearsed it over and over and over and I'm sure the studio was going crazy. But I've done that where I rehearse and rehearse and rehearse and rehearse and they're saying, "Are we going to shoot? It's 3:00!" So he rehearsed it over and over and then he finally did about three takes of it. But essentially that was it. And in one day he just tore out 8–12 pages. He used those restrictions to say, "OK, let's do it a new way," right? Instead of [mimicking a 1st AD] "New deal, new deal – re-light, new deal," you know, he did it all in one take. And that's the one he did on the very first day of shoot. Showed them: "Fuck you guys. I can do it." And he did it a whole new way because of those restrictions.

Shooting The Muppets themselves – like moviemaking itself – is limiting because they have no legs. So I learned a great deal from that, from Jim [Henson] because there is no master shot with the Muppets. No wide, there's no wide master. It doesn't exist because there are no legs to shoot. They've got to always be shot waist-up. And you've got to be careful in your framing because if you shoot a waist-up shot and you're too wide, then all of a sudden you got too much headroom in the frame.

With the Muppets, if there's a prop, say somebody like Kermit, needs to pick up a phone, he can't – not possible. What you're going to do is you cut, switch angles, switch frame sizes, attach the phone, and then he starts talking with it. So there are tremendous limitations with the Muppets and I can go on and on and on, but that's what makes it fun, too, you know? I mean, it's the limitations when you shoot the Muppets that really makes it exciting.

I think for the Muppets – or anyone else for that matter, if they're doing it the right way – those restrictions are a positive. Muppets ... their gestalt, as you talk about, is created by the shots. In other words, instead of a master shot where Kermit walks in and picks up a phone and dials and puts it back down and has a drink of water and leaves, anybody can do that in a master; broken up into shots. For shooting The Muppets, that's probably six cuts. And that cutting creates a rhythm – and you are able to help create a comedic rhythm that way. In the cutting we have more control in the comedic rhythm. But in a mastershot, of course, you have no control. You just gotta do it over and over and over again until it feels right.

I remember when On What About Bob, Richard Dreyfus's character was so angry and was at the top of the stairs during a birthday party, and he had to dive on to Bill [Murray] from like fifteen feet up and people are saying, "Oh, they're going to have to get a stunt man to do that." And because of my training from Jim [Hensen], I knew I can do it with different cuts. I can do it as he starts, then shoot him flying over camera, then I can shoot him landing, you know, as opposed to getting a lot of money and doing it for real with a stunt person. You make it illusory. That is what I was taught with Muppets.

Which was vital with Yoda. George Lucas had no idea how to do Yoda, you know ... it was like a whole thing was resting on this one character and he had no fucking idea how to do it. What I mean is, he didn't know what its setup was going to be. They didn't know if it was going to be a puppet ... if it was animation. They didn't know nothing. And so, you know, he came to Jim [Henson]and Jim suggested me, and he had Stuart [Freeborn] making it. And I think they didn't understand what could be done with the character. They just figured a puppet? Are you kidding me? And it's not the puppets, it's what you do with them.

As the director, Irvin Kershner said, "OK, Yoda's going to pretend he's a little elf in the beginning," and me, the performer, has to prep that. But that's all you can do. You can't do any more than that. That's your limitation – you're only setting up for one action as opposed to Yoda in Dagobah in the hut where now we have a set where I can do much more. But even in there, there's limitation because Yoda has no legs. You really have to know technique. You've got to know your shots and your angles and edit in your head how it's going to be at the end. Anything's allowed in film as long as the intent is pure for the characters and story. I think what is the heart and soul of it is you either try to impose your will on something or you let the heart and soul of it grow and tell you what to do.

With The Muppets you have to prep each shot very well; where the holes need to be cut, for instance. So you'll see a full body, a character sitting on a chair, but you, the performer, are underneath with your arm through it. And so the limitations are vast once you're there because you can't do anything physical – you have to depend on the dialog and your body attitude. You can't – there's nothing physical you can do because you're stuck in a hole, as opposed to if I'm doing a talkshow show, or if I'm doing something where the frame is where I can move around in, then you're, you're cool.

When I shot Little Shop of Horrors, I didn't have the money to do the job right. And I went over budget like crazy. That was a situation where nobody had ever made a talking plant that weighed a ton and sang fast patter. It was impossible, the physics wouldn't allow that. And so that's the limitation. What the fuck am I going to do? You just work with talented people and get ideas.

The real breakthrough was when I and Lyle Conway – who designed the plant, and was in charge of it, everything – were rehearsing with a dummy plant earlier on and we still didn't know how to make it go faster. And we were using videotape at that time to record. And so we recorded it, regular speed. And then we rewound it. And as it went rewinding, I said, "Holy shit – it's talking fast, it's going fast!" And that's what opened it up for me. So we experimented with frame-rates: if we shot at an X amount of speed and tried different speeds, then it would look like it was singing the song that Levi Stubbs had recorded. But in order to do that, we also had to compromise and have Rick [Moranis] go slow. Rick had to move slowly when he was with the plant – he could not sing regular speed because the plant was the focus. I had to shoot 18 or 16 frames per second when it was a plant, and Rick needed to go slow enough so the plant could look like it was going fast once projected at 24 frames per second. But we were free, when it was the plant alone without Rick, to shoot at 12 frames, and then when it was Rick alone we could shoot at regular 24 frames. But when you have a limitation like that, you have to figure it out and fortunately, that fast rewind was the breakthrough.

In terms of giving notes to actors, I think it depends. Michael Caine told me that when he and Sean Connery were doing a Houston film, The Man Who Would Be King, Houston never gave directions to him. He came to Michael only once; Michael had said something about his character Peachy, and Houston came over and said, "Peachy wouldn't say that." And that's about all he ever said.

I've learned to be as short as possible. This is not a time to give acting lessons, especially dealing with people who are of that caliber. But no matter what I do, I just come in and say as few words as I possibly can. Sometimes I won't say a thing. And sometimes when I come in I'll be as judicious as possible and come through the back door. I mean, I will say things that will hopefully spark things to happen, as opposed to look for results. You say to somebody who's talking slowly, you say, "Listen, your cab's outside, your plane is about to take off of at the airport. You've got to get there because it's your mother's funeral," you know, or whatever it is. And I'm not joking about this, but I use sex whenever I can. I mean, it works all the time. It's like in The Indian In the Cupboard. I had this young actor man, Vincent Kartheiser – actually he was also in Mad Men – and he was 14 or something like that, and he had to run down the stairs fast and open the front door of his house. He just wasn't running fast enough. And I said faster. And then I finally said, "OK, look, there's this girl from high school and you can't wait to bone her. And she's at the door." And I yelled, "Action." And then he just took off like a shot. [laughs] I'm serious, I'll use it. Anything that's a sparkplug. It's going through the back door and all you do is create a sparkplug, you know, and get the motor running. That's all.

For The Score, Marlon Brando created a character that I didn't think worked. Neither did my editor. And so I had to restrict him. And by restricting him, not allowing him to perform the way he wanted, he just was himself. And that's exactly what I wanted.

William Pace:
Sorry to interrupt, but ... how did you limit Marlon to get him to be not what he came with, but to be what you wanted.

Frank Oz:
Because they wouldn't pay him if he didn't.

William Pace:
[Laughs.] OK, that one's going in the book.

Frank Oz:
If he didn't listen to me, they weren't going to pay him. They were going to going to find another actor. But at the same time, it was really my fault for not treating Marlon the way a director should treat an actor. I wasn't nurturing, I was combative. I had heard about The Island of Dr. Moreau and how he had taken over completely. And this was a director who was a tough guy, you know, [John] Frankenheimer. And I

said, "I want Marlon in the role," not because he was Marlon the star, because I thought he'd be great for the role. He's a great actor. But I told myself I will not let him take over my movie. I will not do it. So I was very, very tough. I was tough for the first day and a half. And then I realized, "Oh, fuck, I blew it. I'm too tough on him." I should have nurtured him instead, and supported him and said everything was fine. And I didn't and I lost him after that time. So it was my fault.

In terms of the number of takes I'll shoot, I'll do one take if it's inconsequential, if it's a transition scene. Or I'll do nine takes or four takes or I'll do 12 takes depending on the value of the shot. But the way I do it, I don't necessarily do takes, I do three in a row without stopping the camera, which I think is the best way to do it. For many reasons it's my best tool of all. The first time you yell "Action," the actor has already thought beforehand of what is he or she is going to do. And then if you don't say cut, if you say, "OK … keep rolling and reset " – and the actor knows this ahead of time, then that gives them time to go back and start thinking … but not completely because I say "Action," again. And then the third time I do it, before they have the time to think, I say "Action," and they go on. And that's the best part because they don't think, don't have time to think. And it builds a rhythm. It also gets the fucking director out of the actor's face. Because as a performer, I'm into something and all of a sudden I hear "Cut," and the director comes over and talks to me. I don't want the fucking director to talk to me – let me do what I want to do first, okay? So I think it allows the actor to just do it.

I remember I was doing a scene with Edward Norton for The Score and I got excited and sometimes I'd jump in too soon. We're going for a second or third take and I had a thought about the scene and I started to tell him and he says, "Frank, Frank – can you just let me do what I'm doing first and then talk to me?" And I said, "You're absolutely right Edward, you're absolutely right." And he's right. Let them do it. Let them try it. Let them do it over without fucking getting in their faces. And then come in.

In terms of editing I must say, I cut in my head all the time, so when I'm in the edit room, I know what I have already. But there are surprises all the time, especially as I get to the end of the first cut … I'll be stuck. And what will often happen is I think, "Oh, I need a shot over here. And also this and this shot." And I realize, oh wait a second, if I take this shot out and I take this shot out, I don't need either shot. Just cut from this to this. And often that's what I find – I find you don't need those or any new shots.

And talk about restrictions, every movie I've done, they [used to sell directly] to the airlines and you had to take four or five minutes out of your cut, otherwise they couldn't sell it. And of course, after I did the original edit, I said, "It's great. I can't take four or five minutes out of that!" But I have to. And I take four or five minutes out … and never notice them. And that made it better, or made those cuts better because I realized I didn't need them.

You don't need everything you think you need – however, there are things you need that you may not have. And the biggest thing you need is signposts, emotional signposts and story signposts along the way. If you missed one of those signposts, you're going to confuse the audience. So the most important thing is get those signposts that are railings, whatever you want to call them, for the emotional and storytelling elements. Once you have those, you don't need the other stuff as much.

But with Muppet Guys Talking, that was a documentary? Fuck. I mean, it was the first time I realized, you know, that it's a whole different edit – in a script, you're editing to a story; in a documentary you're trying to find a story to edit. It was much harder than any other editing I've ever done. You consider it's only five white people sitting down talking in a room. [laughing] It was hard. Thank God we got the [archival] clips.

We [Frank, producer Victoria Labalme and editor Zana Bochar] had to work for a long time. We whittled and whittled and whittled and whittled, you know. Same thing with In And Of Itself. You know, I had an idea using the footage, and it didn't work, and we just said, "Fuck it. Let's just let the film tell us what to do." And there the juice came.

As for working in Hollywood … I read a biography of a Cuban filmmaker who was very well known, Nestor Almendros, and he did like 60 movies in Cuba, all low budget, and he said that when he came to the Hollywood he was never as creative again because there's too much money.

The more money you have, the more you feel responsible and the safer you become. It's not good. I shot Stepford Wives, and I had all the money, a ridiculous amount of money, like over $100 million. And it didn't feel good at all. It's the bloated weight of a Macy's Day balloon that you're directing with all these people holding the lines down below; it's not as much fun as going down the street just holding a balloon. The worst part of that is it's not fun – it's a lumbering beast; it's not moviemaking to me. It's not making a movie where I can play with the actors and I can have jokes and whatever. It's the limitations that make it exciting to me. You can take more chances with less. That's really where it is. It takes an amazing filmmaker like a Kubrick to have that much money and still do something extraordinary. I'm not saying you can't do it, but I know I don't enjoy it.

That's why I loved doing Death At a Funeral next, because it brought me back to my old days – it was a joy to go and do a $10 million movie. For me, that's low budget. I was looking for something to go back to regular filmmaking with just people and sets and locations. And it was a joy because I had limitations. Because I knew I had a finite amount of time and it wasn't a studio where I could just get more money if I really needed to. It was a joy to work with limitations; to do something that has nothing do with money and you realize, "Oh, shit, I don't have money for it." If you don't have the money, you just figure it out and it's much more exciting.

Although you always have to prep, you know – people don't prep the right way. And if you prep and you have a low budget, you prep enough, you can do great work. It's really the prep, that's what it's about. And the prep is what really helps your restrictions and ambitions, in my opinion.

Oz initially thought he would become a journalist and his passion for that craft still shows as he is infinitely curious about everything and – if one is not careful – will find themselves the one being interviewed.

Let me ask you – what is the best thing about restrictions for you as a filmmaker?

William Pace:
Oh … well, not to flatter you –

Frank Oz:
Please do.

William Pace:
[Laughs.] But the way you described it was exactly how I feel. For instance … in the first feature film Tom [Rondinella] and I made, we had an incident where we had to suddenly – halfway through production – cut about a dozen pages out of the script in order to finish on time and budget. Tom was directing and I was a co-producer on a feature we wrote. We seemed to be doing well, but one day the production manager says to me, "Tom just gave me his complete shot list – why don't you look at it and see where we are in terms of our schedule?" I said, "OK," and I sat down for a couple of hours to look it all over. When I finally came back to her office, I was kind of white in the face. And she goes, "What's wrong?" "We're almost two weeks behind!" According to my calculations, we would need around two more weeks to shoot all the pages and shots that were left, but our end date was the Monday before Thanksgiving so there was no way that was going to happen. Besides the film was supposed to take place in summer and we were already hosing snow off the ground! So Tom and I went off and, I think we cut 12 pages. I'm not really sure, something like that. We created this new scene, or we exchanged and compacted several scenes into one big one that had a wild physical special effects gag in it. And then Tom, myself, the production manager, the director, the DP, and Scottie Buckler, who was the gaffer (who went on to work with Spielberg on *Schindler's List*), we all got into a room the night before the shooting of this new scene that's supposed to bridge everything we cut, and I remember thinking, "How the hell are we going to pull this off!?" But everybody worked as a team to figure it out and make it happen and you know …

Frank Oz:
You felt the juice.

William Pace:
Yes! I did! And when I watch that scene now, I see all that flop-sweat and caffeine and craziness gel into something that became one of the strongest moments in the

film. And then I think, "Oh, my God, what if we had got our way, you know, got to shoot everything we wanted? We wouldn't have this!" So that's what I find truly exciting — seeing something you didn't initially see and then seeing the potential of it when forced to rise to a challenge.

Frank Oz:
Absolutely true. And I also find that the students I've talked to in various places, Chapman, New York University, etc., they think there's one way to do it. I think they're taught to do in a certain way and it's just doesn't really happen that way. There's nothing but obstacles in the way every time you shoot a movie.

William Pace:
Right. And that's a reason I enjoy leading these short films I do with students; one, just showing them the craft and, you know, you really got to treat this as … you can't just run and gun. You need to plan, you need to figure this out. But that doesn't mean you can't all of a sudden have a new idea and everybody work together to make it happen.

Frank Oz:
That's the idea of prep — to be so prepped, you can throw it away and do what you want because you know it's behind there the whole time.

William Pace:
Yeah. The latest film I did with them, the coolest and most interesting shot in it, I didn't have planned when I walked in that day, I didn't have it in my head.

Frank Oz:
What caused it?

William Pace:
The usual — I had too many shots and not enough time.
[Both laugh.]
I needed to combine shots and these kids had just started learning to use a dolly and they were kind of getting confident. And I was like, all right, all right — you think that's fun? Let's try this. Let's do a dolly and a 360° pan. And then the dolly operators, they're going to have to lie flat on the floor as we pan over them, then get right back up and continue pulling. And you see the kids' eyes go wide and say, "We can't do that!" And I'm like, "Can't we? Let's find out." You know, that's what's so fun.

Frank Oz:
Yeah, that is so much fun.

William Pace:
Yeah. Because you push them further than they realize they could go. And then it opens up their eyes to, "What? Oh, we can do this!?"

Frank Oz:
Oh, yeah, exactly right. Exactly. That's the joy, the juice.

GABBY SUMNEY

10.8 Interview Excerpts with Gabby Sumney

Gabby Sumney (Any Pronouns) is an Experimental Media Artist and Cinematographer who makes films, videos, prints, and expanded cinema works that explore issues of race, migration, sexual orientation, gender identity, and ability status. Gabby is also an Assistant Professor of Film Production at the Pennsylvania State University and the creator of This Week in Experimental, a weekly newsletter focused on providing resources to experimental artists seeking creative, intellectual, and exhibition opportunities.[2]

Ingrid Stobbe:
Gabby, every artist has a journey of finding their landing spot, and the area in which they feel they have found a home in expressing themselves – we can call it a genre, a phase of production that speaks to them in a particularly provocative way. Can you speak to us about your own path, and how you feel you found your home in filmmaking - perhaps with a special nod to the twists and turns that didn't work out, and illuminated your road, albeit not necessarily visibly at that moment?

Gabby Sumney:
Filmmaking didn't occur to me as an option until I was 15 or 16. I was a theater kid at that point, and I was planning to study English Literature in college with an eye toward teaching and/or writing. At the start of my junior year, our new Theatre Arts teacher, Kimberly Bledsoe, was telling us about her art practice. I knew her as the leader of a comedy troupe in town, but she told my class of Theatre III students that she was a filmmaker working on her third/fourth short film, and she said that at the end of her career she hoped to be looking at a shelf filled with her film work. I don't think as a working-class Black kid living in North Carolina it ever occurred to me that I could make a film. That was something that happened in Southern California among the rich, famous, and well connected. When I told my dad about it, he told me to ask if she needed help on set during the summer. "Even if you just hold a light, you'll learn definitely learn something." I never got to hold a light for a production, but I did start picking her brain on what it takes to make a film, and I started researching college programs in North Carolina. My dad was really excited for me thinking that worst-case scenario, I could end up working on a tv crew running a camera or something. My mom would have preferred I sought more stable career avenues. I compromised with her by attending a film program at a state school with other options instead of the conservatory with a film program.

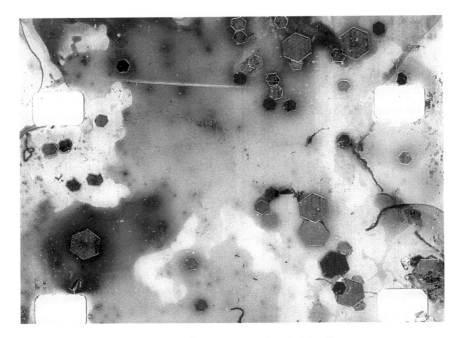

FIGURE GS.1 Still from *Rainbow Dragon*, by Gabby Sumney.

I started asking questions about getting into the film program as soon as I got to UNC Wilmington with the intention of becoming the next Spike Lee, but I was quickly exposed to ways of working and making films that I could have never dreamed of. My first semester with Dr. James Kreul, I watched film from cinemas all over the world and the only films we watched from the US & UK weren't like any film I'd ever seen. I'd come to learn about experimental filmmaking starting with that class, and I'd eventually let that mode and documentary swallow me whole. Around my junior year taking Intermediate Experimental Production after already taking the Intermediate Documentary course, I decided that I wanted to go to graduate school and to teach film – it would take me another year or so to decide between teaching filmmaking or film history.

I think what settled me into experimental nonfiction was seeing how many women, people of color, and queer/trans filmmakers found bold, poetic ways to express themselves on screen and in incredibly small crews. I was really put off by the militaristic hierarchy on narrative sets that I was already seeing my peers emulate, and I was disappointed to see how many historically underrepresented people were kept out of key positions during crew calls. Much in the way that plenty of people go to the movies to escape, I wanted my creative work to be a place for me to escape – even if it meant that I was escaping from the way the world is set up to make work about that very world and its inequities. I have very recently added narrative filmmaking back into my art practice by working as a Director of Photography on a feature film in progress, but I'm happy to report that we're finding ways to challenge the ways the crew interacts and the way that the classic hierarchy often functions. We're also a majority– minority crew with most of using being queer/trans, disabled, women, and/or people of color. It's one of the best environments I've ever worked in both inside and outside of film work.

Ingrid Stobbe:
Fantastic. As a film is usually collaborative, though in some genres more than others, can you discuss a project or collaboration that was particularly meaningful to you, and walk us through what about that work was special or important for you in your work as an artist, in the particular areas that you express yourself.

Gabby Sumney:
I'm in an ongoing collaboration with fellow experimental artist, Hogan Seidel. We're doing a play on the Exquisite Corpse – a surrealist technique of contributing to artwork with only partial knowledge of what the previous artist(s) contributed. We both pass back the same strip of film adding layer upon layer until we decide it's done, and then we scan it and edit it together. We started it to test a mode of experimental collaboration I wanted to try with my undergraduate students. I think part of what makes it special is the improvisation that's so key to this mode of collaborating. We can only respond to how the film strip currently looks with more work either adding to or subtracting from the strip in front of us. We don't tell each other what we've done of how we've achieved that look, nor do we ask for permission to alter various parts. I think it works in part because Hogan and I know each other so well and really engage with filmmaking in the same ways with many of the same reference points. When we started this project, we both lived in Boston, but now we both live in different places far away from each other; so, some of what makes this collaboration so special is that it gives us a structured, regular reason to spend time together working toward the same goal.

Ingrid Stobbe:
What is a specific limitation/restriction you have encountered in your work, that seems to present consistently or in a particular noteworthy instance that impacted you?

Gabby Sumney:
Since we first entered COVID time in 2020, one of the biggest restrictions/limitations I've encountered is access to analog tools to make my work. When I started teaching, I worked somewhere with a ton of access to shared analog and digitizing tools that were supported by a staff of people and worked with by experts working on an analog film at an elite level. Basically, I could book time on an Optical Printer and have access to at least two people at any given time with more knowledge of that machine than I had. I had planned an entire film around using that machine and the expertise around me when suddenly it was dangerous to share

space with other people – particularly as someone who is immune-compromised. I had to really rethink the way that I work and how I can still make the work that speaks to me without sinking all my money into it.

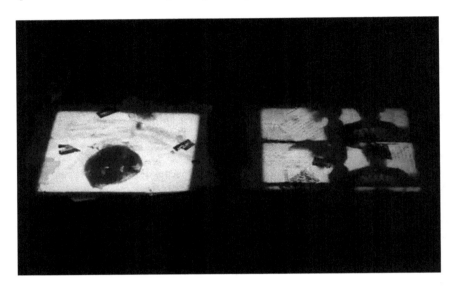

FIGURE GS.2 Stills from *Rituals*, by Gabby Sumney 2016.

Ingrid Stobbe:
How did you deal with it/overcome it?

Gabby Sumney:
I've had to get a little scrappy to overcome this lack of access, and my diminished access to public equipment. Luckily, I had some of the necessary gear and know how to experiment with some workflow solutions. These solutions do change the overall look and feel of the work, but I think those changes reflect the world we live in and bring that world back into the work. As part of my hand-painted film practice, I take high-quality scans of sections to turn into prints for friends and family. Using that same scanner, I've been working with Hogan Seidel to come up with a way we can use our photo flatbed to create animation scans that in some ways are higher quality and more legible that the scans we typically work with to show our analog work digitally. It's an ongoing project, but I think Hogan might have really figured out the registration issues we've been working with for the past two years.

Ingrid Stobbe:
How was the outcome different from a project where you did not encounter any significant limitations/restrictions – if there was a project in which that occurred?

Interviews With Working Artists **161**

Gabby Sumney:
When I compare this work around and the projects that have come from (and are coming from) this hybrid process with projects that were more purely analog, I can see some growing pains and some real delights. Ironically, this hybrid process has slowed me down because it's iterative. That said, I love the look the hybrid process has given me. Since I'm working with a photo scanner at a high DPI, there's greater detail and clarity in these scans. This comes with the tradeoff of the clear digital artifact involved, but so far I think it's worth it.

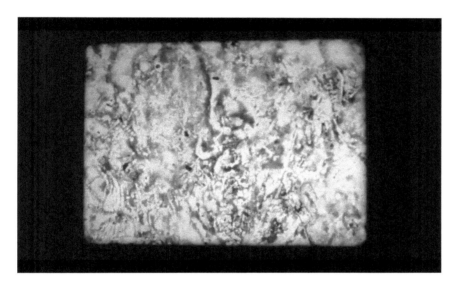

FIGURE GS.3 Still from *Turqoise*, by Gabby Sumney 2016.

Ingrid Stobbe: Do you look for ways to create "built-in" limitations into a project in order to give yourself something to "push against" in the creative process?

Gabby Sumney:
I absolutely impose restrictions and limitations on myself! I think of project planning for experimental projects as building a sandbox. I can do anything I want to within the confines of that sandbox. I can dig a tunnel or a whole; I can build a castle or mound; I can simply enjoy the feeling of the sand.

A quick example: I'm working on a short experimental documentary about my paternal grandmother who died in 2018. All the footage in that piece was either collected in Iceland or animation assembled using tape transfers from a magazine I picked up while I was there in early 2020. It's important to me that the film really has a sense of that place since we were both there about 50 years apart. I wanted to really focus on our shared/separate sense of being tourists in the same place when we were around the same age as young, married people.

Notes

1 https://www.shaunclarke.com/
2 Gabby Sumney, www.GabbySumney.com, accessed June 18, 2022.

PT. V
Addendum

11
SPARE SCENES FOR YOUR USE AND PRACTICE

```
          SPARE SCENE #1
            "It's Time"

              1
    I think it's time.

              2
    Time?

              1
    Yeah.

              2
    For what?

              1
    You know.

              2
    I do?

              1
    Yes.
        (beat)
    Right?
```

                    2
            (beat)
Yeah.

                    1
All right, then.

                    2
Now?

                    1
Now.

                    2
            (beat)
Now.

                    1
You're sure?

                    2
Yeah, why not?

                    1
That's convincing.

                    2
No, yeah – I'm sure.

                    1
All right, let's go.

                    2
Fine.

SPARE SCENE #2
"I Can't"

        1
I can't.

        2
You can't what?

        1
You know.

        2
   (beat)
Really!?

        1
Yeah, sorry.

        2
Now!?

        1
Yeah ... no.

        2
Great timing!

SPARE SCENE #3
"That's It"

     1
That's it?

     2
That's it.

     1
Oh.

     2
Oh?

     1
Yeah.

     2
What?

     1
Nothing.

     2
Right.

     1
I just …

     2
You just …

     1
Nothing.

     2
Nothing.

SPARE SCENE #4
"You Look"

      1
Wow! You look ...

      2
Yes?

      1
You look ... just so ... wow.

      2
Thank you?

      1
No I really mean it.

      2
I know you do it's just that ...

      1
Yeah?

      2
I don't know what you mean.

      1
I mean ... I look at you and ... wow.

      2
Huh.

SPARE SCENE #5
"He Said"

      1
But he said --

      2
No.

      1
But he said --

      2
That's not happening now.

      1
Why?

      2
Because she said --

      1
Wait - now's she's saying?

      2
Yep.

      1
Oh.

      2
Yep.

SPARE SCENE # 6
"That's What Happened"

        #1
That's what happened.

        #2
Wow!

        #1
Yep.

        #2
That's crazy!

        #1
Don't use that word.

        #2
What?
    (pause)
Oh, right.
    (pause)
Still …

        #1
Yeah.

        #2
And they never … ?

        #1
Never.

        #2
Wow.

SPARE SCENE #7
"It's Happening"

             1
It's happening.

             2
Again?

             1
Yep.

             2
Unbelievable.

             1
Believe.

             2
But I thought we –

             1
Didn't last.

             2
Oh.
    (pause)
So …

             1
Yep.

             2
Then should we …

INDEX

Italicized and **bold** pages refer to figures and tables respectively, and page numbers followed by "n" refer to notes.

accessibility 37, 44, 51, 54, 58, 67, 121
AD *see* assistant director
ADR *see* automated dialogue replacement
Alfred, R. 59n4
Ali, S. 145
amateurism 66–72
American Social History Project, History Matters 36n14
American Union Bank 1920 *21*
Aragon, L. 13
Arzner, D. 18–19, *19*, 23, 61
Asner, J. 26–27
assistant director 5, 6
audience 4, 5, 14, 16, 23, 24, 27, 37, 45, 65, 68, 72, 107–108, 112, 126, 128, 138, 141, 143, 146, 154; emotions 34; movie experience 3; screen colour 32; sensibilities 25
automated dialogue replacement 88
Aviation 20

Babiolakis, A. 36n6
Baird, J.L. 52
Banton, T. 30
Barrish, S.: acting 126–129; creative process 129; film directing 128–129; interview 126–129
Baumgarten, M. 36n20

Beatty, T. 133
Beckett, S. 85
Bergman, I. 30
Betamax 51
Binoche, J. 128
Birbiglia, M. 126
Bird, B. 141
Bitoun, R.E. 36n18, 32
black and white cinematography: color intensities 32–33; multiple visual languages 33; technicolor 31, *31*; techniques and innovations 32; technology 30; three-strip process 31, *31*; TV 32
Bledsoe, K. 157
Blockbuster 57–58, *57*
Boccioni, U. *12*
Bochar, Z. 154
body language 17, 82, 87
boom pole 18–19
Bow, C. 18–19, *19*
Boyle, W.S. 49
Brando, M. 76, 152
Breton, A. 13
British Royal National Theatre 85
British Society of Cinematographer 135
budget 3, 9, 54, 58, 67–68, 71, 120, 122, 128, 129, 148, 151, 154, 155
Burton, T. 15

The Cabinet of Dr. Caligari 14–16, *15*
Caine, M. 76, 152
camcorder 50, 51, 54, 54
Camera Obscura 37–38, *38*, 59n1
Cameron, J. 63
Capone, A.G. *20*
Cardiff, J. 136
Card, L. *15*
cartridge 48
cast 6, 7, 40, 88, 138, 146, 147
Castelnuovo, N. 33
Cathode Ray Tube Television Set 53, *53*
CCD chip *see* Charged Coupled Device
celluloid-film 42, 47, 56, 59n4, 122
censorship 19, 27, 29
CGI *see* computer-generated imagery
Charged Coupled Device 48–51, *49*
Children of Men 95
Cinderella (1951) 65, 142
cinema 10, 11, 14–17, 31, 32, 45, 58, 70, 82, 94, 119, 121, 157, 158; censorship 19–30; development 19; language 16
cinematographer 3, 17, 32, 58, 129, 131–136, 157
cinematography 31, 32, 114, 131, 135, 136, 138
clarity 6, 7, 9, 143, 161
Clarke, S. 129–135
climactic sequence 3, 6, 7, 95
code-stretching 23
color: contrast 33, *33*; intensities 32–33, *33*; photograph 52; triads 53;
See also black and white to color
Comfortable Working Height 137
computer-generated imagery 62–64
Conway, L. 151
Cook, D.A. 59n5
costumes 15, 22, 25, 29, 30, 34, 35, 82; designers 30; schemes 34
Covid-19 pandemic 121–122, 140, 159
crew 6, 7, 69, 73, 121, 148, 157–159
Cubism 12
Curtis, O. 135–140
Curtis, T. *29*, 30
CWH *see* Comfortable Working Height

Dadaism 12, 96
Dadaists 16
dada movement 14
Daguerre, L.J.M. 38
daguerrotype *39*
Dance, Girl, Dance (1940) 23
Dark Crystal 75

DaVinci, L. 120
Davis, B. 30
Deakins, R. 136
Death At a Funeral 138
Demme, J. 83
Deneuve, C. 33
DeNiro, R. 76
Deren, M. *67*; amateur artists 67; artistic freedom 68; camera tricks 71; female filmmaker 67; filmaking skill 67–71; 3-lens Bolex 70; time freedom 68
dialogue 17, 19, 29, 46, 53, 68, 83–90, 93, 95, 129
Diamond, I.A.L. 29
Dickson Experimental Sound Film 17
Dickson, W.K.L. 43
digital imaging 48, 51
director 3–7, 18, 22, 73, 77, 122, 126–132, 136, 137, 139, 140, 145–149, 151–153, 159; AD 5; audience emotions 34; cinematographers 59; DoP 5; producers 58; time and money 6
Director of Photography 5, 129, 135, 136, 139, 159
Docter, P. 63–65, 87, 107–108, 140–144
Dogme-95 movement 54–56, 77
DoP *see* Director of Photography
Dreyfus, R. 150
Duchamp, M. *13*
dynamic ranges 54, 58, 96, 122

Eastmancolor 32
Eastman, G. 40
Eastman Kodak 32, 33, 40, 42, 47
Eccles, R. 91
Edison, T. 42, 43
editing 71, 75, 82, 83, 91, 95–97; filmmaker 106; in production 112–115; sequences 16; in storytelling 109–112; techniques 16
editor 18, 70, 83, 110–113, 115
e-resources 108
Ernst, M. 13
Evil Dead 77
evolutions: art and World war I 11–14, *12, 13*; black and white to color 30–35; cinema censorship 19–30; Hays Code 19–30; isolation and storytelling 10–11; pre-sound to post-sound 16–19; World Wars 10–11
Expressionists 16
Exquisite Corpse 110–111, 159

Fairley, R. 50
Farnsworth, P.T. 53
fiber-optic networking 57
Fichandler, Z. 146
Field, A.N. 36n5
film 18, 23, 30, 33, 40–44, 54–57, 64, 68, 81–83, 106–110; digital 54; elements 40; grammar and language 16; innovations 41; persistence of vision 40; shooting 6; time and money 6
filmmakers: amateur 68; audience 47; dump truck approach 94; early-stage 82; edits, cuts and shots 109; e-resources 108; freedom 69; geography 4, *4*; goals 109; open/spare scene 95; shots 96; styles 61; thinking 9
filmmaking: blocking/shooting of scenes 8; device 43; dialogue 87; editing 94; genres 8; geography 3, 4, *4*, 6; length 8; post-production process 106; resources 8; story structure 8
film production 10–35
footage 50, 94, 112–115
Fountain, photograph *13*
framing 94–96; continuity of cuts 99–100; edges 99–100, *101*; digital funcationalities *105*; multiple directionality *102*, *104*; sample paintings *103*; lensing, maximizing 99–100; reversed exquisite corpse 110–111; spatiality 99–100
free-lensing 98
Frymus, A. 59n9
Futurism *12*, 12

Game of Thrones 58–59
geography 3, 4, *4*, 6
German Expressionism 11, 14–16, 36n4
Get Your Man (1927) 18
Gibson, W. 92
Gilpin, C. 47
Gish, L. 17
Golden Girls 121
Gone With the Wind 31
Goodwin, H. 40, 42
Gosling, R. 128
"Great Depression History" 36n10
The Great Train Robbery 46
Grimberg, R. 70, 77n3

haiku 91–93
Haines, B. 30
Hall, G. 144–148

Harding, W.G. 47
Haring, K. 136
Harlem's Gem Theater 47
Harlow, O. 50
Harries, S. 60n19
Hartley, M. *13*
Harvey, N. 126
Hastings, R. 56
Hays code 29; costume 25; crimes against the law: illegal drug traffic 24; liquor use 24; methods of crime 24; murder 24; dances 26; guidelines, motion pictures 22; Hays, W.H 19; innovation 27; locations 26; national feelings 26; obscenity 25; principles 24; profanity 25; religion 26; repellent subjects 26–27; set of rules 19; sex: adultery 24; children's sex organs 25; miscegenation 25; passion scenes 25; perversion 25; seduction or rape 25; titles 26; vulgarity 25
Hays, W.H. 21–23, *22*
Hemmingway, E. 91–93
Henson, J. 72, 73, 75
Hiltzik, M. 35n1
Hollywood 11, 23, 54, 66, 70, 122, 154
Hoover, H. 21
Hosch, W.L. 60n20
House of Cards 57
House UnAmerican Activities Committee 11
HUAC *see* House UnAmerican Activities Committee
Hughes, H. 26
Hulu 121
Huston, J. 32

innovation: black and white to color 30–35; cinema censorship 19–30; digital 121; film 18; Hays Code 19–30; screenwriting 17; shot length 17; unexpected limitations 10
inspiration 11, 15, 119, 141
instruments: DSLR camera 97; group engagement 98; lens whacking 97; optical device 96; tilt-shift lens 97

Jaws 77, 140
Jazz 20, 127
The Jazz Age 20
The Jazz Singer 16–17
Jewell, R.B. 31

Jolly Dolly 94–96
Jolson, A. 16
Jurassic Park 141

Kalmus, H. 30
Kazaan, E. 11
Keaton, B. 16
Kershner, I. 151
Kidman, N. 76
Kinetograph 43, 44
Kinetoscope 43–44, *43*
Kit, B. 122
Kreul, J. 158

Labalme, V. 154
At Land 67
Lang, F. 14
language 16, 17, 33, 34, 46, 82, 110, 149
Lasseter, J. 141
Last Night In Soho 139
Lee, S. 77, 158
Lemmon, J. *29*, 30
Le Prince, L. 42, 43
Levenson, J. 50
Lewis, M. 18, 23, 36n11
lighting 15, 35, 55, 119, 128, 140
Lilyhammer 57
Little Shop of Horrors 75
Love and Death on Long Island 136
Lucas, G. 150
Lumière Brothers 44, *44*

makeup 15
Manhattan Cockatil (1928) 18
Marey, E.-J. 42
The Martini Shot 77
Martin, S. 76
Matter of Life and Death 136
Maxwell, J.C. 52
McKay, C. 83
McKee, R. 88
McLaren, N. 133
Mekas, J. 70
Méliès, G. 45, 46
Meshes of the Afternoon 67, 70–71, *71*
Metcalfe, L. 127
microphone 18–19
Midler, B. 76
Miller, A. 70
mockumentary 126
Monroe, M. *29*, 30
Moran, M. 126
Motion Picture Production Code 23

movie making 3, 48
Movie Ratings System 26–27
Muppets 149; characters 73; comedy style 75; mobility 73; penguin waiter *73*; puppet show 74; TV show 72
Murnaur, R.W. 14
Murphy, E. 76
Murray, B. 76
Muybridge, E. 41, *41*, *42*

The National World War I Museum and Memorial 11n2
negative film 30–33, 39–41, 66, 138, 144
Netflix 57, 121, 122
Niépce, J. 38
nitrocellulose 40
Nobel Prize 49
Nolan, C. 59
non-verbal communication 87–91
Norton, E. 76, 153

Old Ironsides (1926) 18
O'Neill, A. *98*
onscreen exposition 87–91
On The Waterfront, film 11
On With The Show! 1920 31
open scene 84
Orry-Kelly 29–30
Oscars 30, 136, 140
Oz, F. 62, 72–76, 106, 138, 149–157

Pace, B. 126
Pace, W. 107–108, 148, 152, 155–156
PCA *see* The Production Code Administration
The Perfect Dancer 135
perspectives 7, 16, 45, 62, 65, 72, 108, 111, 112, 120, 143
Phonofilm 17
photography *13*, 16, 37–43, 47, 132, 135, 139, 159
Picture of Spatial Growths-Picture with Two Small Dogs 14
Pixar Animation Studios 62–65, *64*, 87, 108, 140, 141
pixels 37, 51, *52*, 53, 56, 58, 81, 122
Porter, E. 45–46
post-production 81, 96, 106, 112, 120
pre-production 81–83, 106, 120, 139
producer 6, 17, 22, 23, 58, 70, 139, 140, 154
production 3, 6, 7, 9, 82, 96, 120, 138, 146, 155, 157; amateur 68; editing

112–115; film 10–35; value 82–83, 120, 139
The Production Code Administration 23

Rabinowitz, S. 36n7
Raimi, S. 77
Randolph, M. 56
The Red Shoes 136
Reichenback, H. 40
reshooting 129, 139
Ring, T. 36n16
Rivera, J. 141
Romano, R. 127
Roosevelt, F.D. 21

scene relevancy 82
School Daze 77
Schulberg, B. 11
Schwitters, K. 14
Scorsese, M. 59, 95
screenplay 18, 29, 81, 84, 86, 90; haiku 91–93; non-verbal communication 87–91; onscreen exposition 87–91
screenwriting 11, 17, 27, 82, 84–88, 91, 92; deets 86–87; goals 87
Seidel, H. 110, 159, 160
sex scenes, Hays Code: adultery 24; children's sex organs 25; miscegenation 25; passion scenes 25; same-sex relationship 30; seduction or rape 25; sex hygiene 25; sex perversion 25; white-slavery 25
Shakespeare, W. 85
Sharf, Z. 60n23
Sheldon, R. 49
Sherman, C. 70
shooting 3–8, 55, 57, 68, 94, 96, 129, 136, 138, 149, 155; climactic sequence 7; close-ups 77; film 6; luxury 72; multiple locations 121; truck 4, *4*
Shyamalan, M.N. 15
Silence of the Lambs (1991) 83
silver chloride 38
silver halide 38
silver-plated sheets 38
Singing in the Rain 17
Sleepwalk With Me 129
Smith, G. 49
Society of Independent Artists exhibit 1917 *13*
Some Like it Hot (1959) 27–30, *28*, *29*

Sony 50, 136
sounds 5, 8, 10, 23, 30, 48, 55, 56, 62, 82, 88, 112, 120, 129, 140, 143; filmmaking 16; pre-sound to post-sound 16–19; recording 61
spare scene 84–86, 92, 95, 165–172
Spielberg, S. 59, 95, 141
sprockets 42
Stanton, A. 141
Starling, C. 83
Stars Wars 75
Stieglitz, A. *13*
Stock Market 20
storyboards 4, 65, 100, 120, 142, 143
storytelling 9, 81; editing 109–110; elements 8; subjectivity 109–110; topic imposition 109–110
Stranger Things 58
streaming platform 56–59, 122
Stubbs, L. 151
A Study in Choreography for the Camera 67
Sumney, G. 110, 157–162, *158*, *160*, 162n2
Super 8 48–49, *48*, 50, 60n11
Surrealism 12, 14, 70, 96
Surrealists 16

Talbot, W.H.F. 39, 41
Tan, M. 60n21
tape-based consumer media 50
tapes 48, 50, 51, *51*, 75, 151, 161
Technicolor 31, *31*
Television 32, 53, 58, 62, 75, 90, 91, 126, 127, 137–139, 148, 157
televisor 52
Ten Nights in the Barroom 47
Terminator 2 63
theater 16, 21, 26, 32, 47, 59, 121, 126–129, 144–146, 149, 157; film 18; instruments 17; language 46
The Wizard of Oz 31
Thomas, D. 70
three-strip process 31, *31*
Time Versus Money 131, *132*
Tompsett, M.F. 49
Tonks, H. 13
toolsets 8, 110
A Touch of Evil 149
Toy Story 1: CGI 62–66; filmmaking process 62; gestation period 63; stylistic and practical choices *64*, 65; Tin Toy 63, *64*
Toy Story 2 141

Treaty of Versailles Germany 1919 14
A Trip to the Moon 46
Tron 62

The Umbrella's of Cherbourg, 1964 33–35, *34, 35*
Unemployed men, soup kitchen 1920 *20*
Unique Forms of Continuity in Space 12

Vaudevillian Nickelodeons, movie theater 47
VHS *see* Video Home System
video: accessibility 54; camera recorder 50; CCD 49–51, *50*; celluloid structure 122; color TVs 53; and digital imaging 49; Dogme-95 Chastity 55–56; film frames 55; pixel 51, *52*, 53; streaming 57–59, 122; Super 8, 48–49, 51; tape systems 49; VHS 48
Video Hom System 48, 51, 52, *52*, 54
Vinterberg, T. 55, 77
Vitaphone 17

Vitascope 47
von Trier, L. 77

Wagner, F. 58
Waiting for Godot, play 85
WALL.E, 140
Weber, L. 23
Welles, O. 95, 149
Wichary, M. *31*
Wiene, R. 14
Wilder, B. 27, 29
The Wild Party (1929) 18–19, *19*, 23
World Wars: art movements 10; Cold War 11; communism 11; expression 11; screenwriting 11; World War I 11–14, *12, 13*; World War II 14, 15
Wright, E. 139

YouTube 95

Zoopraxiscope 41
Zurich 14